THE ART OF LIVING

THE ART OF LIVING

RAHSAAN AKI TAYLOR

J. KENKADE PUBLISHING™

A division of J. Kenkade Enterprises, LLC.

J. Kenkade Publishing
6104 Forbing Rd
Little Rock, AR 72209
www.jkenkade.com
Facebook.com/JKenkade

J. Kenkade Publishing is an imprint of
J. Kenkade Enterprises, LLC.
The J. Kenkade Publishing name and logo
are trademarks of J. Kenkade Enterprises, LLC.

Printed in the United States of America
ISBN 978-1-944486-60-0 (Paperback)
ISBN 978-1-944486-05-1 (eBook)

Dedicated to my first born,
Zi'Yaan Taylor on his 13th birthday.
Happy Birthday son. Daddy loves you.

Acknowledgments

First and foremost, I'd like to thank the Almighty Living God, Who is the head of my life. Like the song says, "I wouldn't have made it without you." I'm not ashamed to say that God is my redeemer, deliverer, provider, rock and shield.

Special thanks to my wonderful mother Mary King—words can't express the prominent affection that I have for you. So from this day forward, I've decided to show you with my actions. Continue to hold on so strong in what you believe in.

To my lovely grandparents, Pearlie Mae Beasley, Ezell Beasley, Rest in Love Vernell Martin— I wouldn't have been born if it wasn't for both of you. Your provision, protection, strength, health, and desires are always being prayed for.

I am proud of my ingenious children Zi'Yaan and Mariyah. I love you. You two are forever my babies. Believe it or not, you are the golden reason why I have survived the struggle. Dj and A'alyssa, I'm writing this book to inspire you all. I never knew that I had hidden talents and gifts until I was compelled to discover them.

To my aspirational sister Shekila, My brilliant brother Keith, phenomenal sister Nioka, and miraculous sister Tichina— I haven't forgotten the good deeds that you have done for me.

To my incredible Aunt Virginia and Aunt Lean; My remarkable cousins Shamika, Tonya, and Sunshine— I appreciate all of you for your helping hands. Keep enjoying life, but don't undermine what is most important.

Much love to my Fans, Spiritual Family, Proofreaders, Editors, Prayer Warriors, Street Team evangelists, Frieda Broadax, Prophetess Clara Davis, women of Power, and everyone else that has prayed for me and gave me words of wisdom and encouragement.

My apologies if your name slipped my mind, but be on the lookout for it in my next novel called "Enough is Enough."

Preface

This book contains quotes that have been harbored, festered, and mustered in my head. Eighty percent of this book was inspired by quotes out of my own great mind, with the rest being common quotes that are used in daily society.

Since we are aware that we are faced daily with challenges that we must conquer and overcome, the best way to solve a problem is to have the tools. Since most of our life sequences begin in the mind, the contents of this book will help you maintain, stay afloat, and/or resolve some of your troubles.

Keep in mind that everything will not happen at once. Every quote and stanza that you read in this book is to be meditated upon day and night until you receive every piece of the puzzles to make it whole. It has been said that the best way to hide anything from someone is to place it inside of a book. Oh, how valuable knowledge is!

These are the jewels that are priceless; but very beneficial, resourceful, enlightening and a sure way to have you high-spirited. In this book, you will find the codes and ingredients to substation what is required to live a prosperous and peaceful life.

ᏟᏰᏋᏕᏡᏒ

Day 1

THINGS AREN'T ALWAYS what they seem to be. I was once talking to this girl and she told me her head was hurting. I asked, "Why does your head hurt?" She replied, "Because of our situation!" So I told her, "You know what your problem is? You want to be the man in this relationship. You want to control my every action and monitor everyone that I come in contact with. I see why your brain is about to blow up! You're worried for nothing. You're concerned about unnecessary things. And all you have to do is relax and be humble. But the main thing is to play your position. A woman by nature is supposed to be submissive to her man. If you don't want to be treated like any woman, then act like a woman and carry yourself like my woman. Don't be around here getting all rowdy for nothing. If you have a problem with me, then come to me and ask what's going on. When you begin to play your part, then I will play mine." She replied, "Ok, I understand. I see." She came to find out that I was merely taking care of business and not messing off. She found out that the female associates were other family members. After all this time, headaches and undercover anger weren't even caused for.

Today, I will recognize that things aren't what they always seem to be. Just because I'm thinking a certain way doesn't mean that my way is rational or logical. Just because a cloud is in the shape of a man or animal doesn't mean it's what it appears to be. It's a cloud. Not a man or animal.

Day 2

SOME THINGS we have no control over! We as humans love for things to be in our control. We want to master the art of every element of life. However, some things are not in our hands. For instance, if we just got our hair done and we are walking down the street on a perfectly sunny day, then all of a sudden it begins to pour down raining: Did we have any control over that? Of course not. Perhaps, the meteorologist even miscalculated that chance of rain on the weather channel. So how would we have known for a split second our hair-do would be ruined? Never think you can subdue everything like sickness, death, world peace, and what a person decides to do or not do. No one can be in every place at one time to protect, provide, or make decisions for others.

Starting this day forward, I will accept that I do not have control over everything. When things begin to go against my might, I will not be overshadowed.

Day 3

THERE are 6 types of Love:

1. *Sexual love-* When you misconstrue love for lust. People live for the sake of pleasure. I believe this is why people who really can't get along stay together. They really don't want the other person to have sex with anyone else.
2. *Brotherly love -* Everyone you like are not meant to be friends. Love them as a sister and brother. However, when people mistake what brotherly love truly is, they begin giving their affection to everyone intimately because they feel special.
3. *Unconditional love-* When you love a person regardless of their condition. You are willing to work situations out and make a natural bond last forever. You turn a death ear to their flaws. It's the type of love that is mentioned in those marriage vows. For better or worse is the key. Through thick and thin. Surviving the good and the bad. Everybody wants the good, but want to run from the bad, or when they get to doing great, they act funny or shady.
4. *Sacrificial love-* Putting your loved ones before you. Jesus Christ is the perfect example of sacrificial love. Most people are not willing to accept a loss so they do not have sacrificial love.
5. *Selfish love-* When everything is about yourself. You don't focus on your spouse's point of views or consider their values. You only see things your way. A lot of people are filled with selfish love and that's why their relationships or friendships don't work out.
6. *Surprising Love-* is when you're basically confused in a relationship. You don't know whether you are going or coming. The expectation of your spouse or friend can never be determined.

I will learn the 6 different types of love and study them.

Day 4

LAZY PEOPLE ARE VISIONLESS PEOPLE and bored people are people who haven't found their purpose for living yet! People with no ambition have never harbored a proposition. A lazy spell has cast upon them and taken away their drive, motivation, and will. They are not go-getters! Lazy people set a poor example for people, especially kids. They ought to develop a dream, vision, or goal and surface to achieve it. Yet, they prefer to lay and sit around. Bored people have nothing to do because they have an idle mind. Usually they end up in mischief because it's true that an idle mind is the devil's workplace. Bored people have never thoroughly focused on their talents and inborn gifts. They don't utilize the substances that they already have to get ahead. If it's only to read an educational or self-help book to put ideas in their head. Instead of being bored, they could do something constructive.

When a lazy spell overshadows me, I will cast it down and become energetic. I will not let myself become bored. I will be constructive, educative, or spend my time wisely. Even if it's only spent with family or love ones.

ଔଓଓଔ

Day 5

SHOOT FOR THE MOON. If you miss, then you are still amongst the stars! Somewhere in space is a gravity field that has a strong push or pull on movements. No matter what you aim for, it's not a 100% certainty that you will hit anything. Just like the force will throw you off track in space, that's exactly how real life is. You can always aim for the best or the biggest achievement but there's no guarantee that you will accomplish that. However, as long as you aim for the biggest point or main attraction, even if you miss your target, you will land somewhere in that area.

Even if I didn't reach my highest peak. I will still find beauty where I'm stationed in life.

Day 6

EVIL is the direct outcome of ignorance. We must understand why it has come upon us and what we must learn from it! Ignorance is another form of not being cognizant...unaware of what is actually happening to you or the people surrounding you. We will all at some point and time become a victim of evil. Evil is inevitable. However, when dirt is thrown upon us or when we are insidiously affected, we must develop some type of understanding to prevent it from happening to us again. Then we must contemplate the lesson within evil. Maybe we put out an unintentional gesture or maybe we were at the wrong place at the wrong time.

I understand that everything I go through is vital in achieving a higher level in life. Yet, if I don't understand why it has come upon me or if I haven't learned from the situation, I will only take that evil test repeatedly until I pass it.

Day 7

WHEN ONE DOOR SHUTS, another one is getting ready to open! When inmates are convicted at trial in a circuit court, they are eligible to appeal their case to Supreme Court. If the Supreme Court shuts them down, then they can go higher to the U.S. district. After affirmation or reversal, they will be challenged in the 8th circuit. That's just like relationships. When one boyfriend or girlfriend steps out of your life, sooner or later a better one may change positions.

I have to know that when a door shuts I am not permanently shut out of all entrances. I only have to be patient and aware until I recognize the new door that opens. Likewise, I must also realize that all doors do not open by themselves. I may have to apply effort to open it. I will not be afraid to explore.

Day 8

IF YOU FAIL TO PLAN, then you plan to fail! You are always planning whether you know it or not. Even if you are not intentionally planning, you are unconsciously planning. For instance, most of the time when you are traveling an unknown area you glance at certain things maybe to admire them. You are not planning to remember that landmark or site. However, if you ever cross it again or if someone mentions it, that landmark or site will re-register in your head even though you never planned on remembering it.

I must recognize that when I don't establish a profound plan. I have already set myself up for failure.

Day 9

PLANNING DESTROYS WORRYING! Just like faith cancels worrying, and on the other note, worrying cancels faith. When you are making plans worries subside. Planning bigger and better things also takes your mind off of the negative issues. It will help you bear or cultivate the problem.

The next time that I begin worrying, I will move my mind to planning and focusing, no matter how strong my mind tries to draw me back to the streets.

Day 10

THERE IS NO PROGRESS without struggle! Everybody in some form or shape must put forth some kind of effort, strength, or muscle if they want to see flourishing results. No matter how hard the push or pull, one must continue to thrive. If you ever heard of "no pain, no gain", then you know exactly what I mean.

Every day I will move towards the mark to reach my dreams, goals, or vision. I understand that hardship will come. However, I must endure through it all.

Day 11

HE WHO SUCCEEDS in establishing himself in the highest virtue brings the whole world to his feet! If you don't believe in yourself, then nobody else will believe in you. But if you carry yourself with confidence, wisdom, and charisma then others will connect with the vibe. Furthermore, when you are in their presence, they will submit or rather fall in suit with the impression that you put out. People in authority carry this affect all the time. Imagine that you are at a job site. For some reason you are not doing what your requirements for the job consists of. Now imagine what happens when your boss enters the room coincidently, everybody appears to be the hardest working person ever. It's the same way when you are in the presence of royalty or someone highly respected such as the president. Once your image is created superior, the inferiors know who they are.

I must realize that I have to be fully established before any one decides to follow me, listen to me, or worship me.

Day 12

THE FUTURE IS NOW. You can tell the kind of life you're going to have in the future by the decisions you are making today! Have you ever heard the saying "Show me your top five friends and I will show you yourself!"? That proverb was created because it is true. People are influenced by their environment as well as the decisions they make. If you choose to hang with people that are miserable, then sooner or later, you will grow miserable. On the other hand, if you decide to hang with cheerful and prosperous people, then eventually their substance will rub off on you. As of right now, whatever you decide to do in life, where you decide to go, or whomever you choose to accompany with will make a major impact on your future. Believe it or not, the next second is the future. So what you decide to do right now and every moment of your life dictates how you will continue to live.

I decide my future in the present.

ଓଃଃଃ

Day 13

RESPONSIBILITY IS REALLY RESPONDABILITY which is the ability to respond to the requirements of your vison. I hear a lot of people say "such and such needs to be about their responsibility." I hear them say that "such and such don't take care of his or her responsibility." True enough we all have our inputs on what someone else's responsibility should pertain to. The question should be, are we reaching our own criteria? Deep down inside we know our heights and our depths. We know that we can proceed further than the length that we have become accustomed to. Yet, we tend to hesitate, procrastinate or hold ourselves back.

The next time I see or hear responsibility, I will know that it pertains to two words. Those words are respond and ability. I must respond in some type of way, preferably by my actions, and my ability is the capabilities inside of me.

Day 14

GOD CANNOT BE UNDERSTOOD by anyone but you! Everyone has a god rather they realize it or not. To some people a basketball is their god. To other money, alcohol, drugs, or people is their god. Whatever they worship, serve, and go out of the way for is their god. However, the god that I mentioned in the above quote is the living God I'm pertaining to. In order to develop a relationship with the true God is through intimacy. Learning to listen to God is a major key. In result, we must recognize what God is and then accept the fact that only spirits can intercede with spirits.

No matter what! It is worth an attempt to understand the living God from whom God is.

Day 15

POWER IS ORGANIZED KNOWLEDGE expressed through intelligent efforts! Power is literally knowing the mastery of the mental. The only way to know is to seek, search, and develop the understanding of knowledge. The key word is "know." Know is the first four letters of knowledge. Not just any knowledge. This particular knowledge has to be significant and orchestrated in a dynamic sequence. Power is the way you carry yourself, think, feel, and act. It's what you bring in and what you put out.

In order to be powerful I must first obtain the highest knowledge of virtue. Then I must diligently apply it sagaciously.

Day 16

YOU HAVE TO KNOW HOW to maneuver between the alternatives of life! Alternatives are merely choices or possibilities that will occur in our life. Every day and any moment, a decision has to be made. Not only one decision is being made, but several decisions. In order to become proficient, we must make awkward moves at times. The ability to maneuver is the art of an acrobat. We have to have the communication and skills of life, such as a ninja would move therein. Maneuvering is not always easy but it must be done.

I have noticed that alternatives and maneuvering gets more difficult as life moves along. My strategy should solely depend on the levels or consequences.

Day 17

MAJORITY OF THE TIME, it is the little things that count! There was once a little girl that lived in a place. Her family was wealthy so they supplied her with everything that they figured would make the little girl happy. She had computers, ipods, diaries, cellphones, friends, and all kinds of the latest toys. The nanny that kept her cooked her meals on request. Candy, ice cream, and sweets was always on hand. Not to mention the prettiest clothing. Both of her parents were hard working people. They made a good and honest living, but to earn their success, it took most of their time, effort and energy at work. They spent close to 14 to 16 hours a day at work. They hardly ever had time for anything. In their mind, as long as their daughter was well taken care of nothing else mattered. Unbeknownst, the little girl only played with high priced toys two or three times before she lost interest in them. She ate so many sweets her belly ached. Her friends were only there to get what they could get out of her. On top of that, she use to rip holes in her expensive clothing because the kids she went to school with couldn't afford her type of designers. She wanted to fit in so she made her self-esteem less fortunate to fit in.

The flipside to this story is that the girl grew up in resentment, unaffectionate, and spoiled. She didn't care about the toys, electronics, and food. What she really wanted was to spend time with her parents. She wanted a hug when her parents were too tired to give her one. She wanted to hear her parents voice when they were too busy to speak. Throughout the years of her growing up they spent millions of dollars on what they thought was for her pleasure or entertainment. However, those big gifts were in vain. All she ever wanted was the simplest things in life.

Pay attention to people's behavior. Just because you smother them with luxurious things doesn't mean it carries more worth than a tiny sentimental gesture.

CSSOSOCR

Day 18

TO SETTLE SOMEONE'S DOUBT, point out the weakness in it! Everyone has doubts. So it is our job to help them over shadow that darkness. For instance, if someone were to second guess whether or not if they should get on an airplane because of their fear of heights, you would go through the channels to subside their doubts. Perhaps you can call the airplane line along with them to assure the plane has been checked for any faults. You let them know how successful landing has been for you, or you let them know that it is quicker to get there by plane or they may be stuck in the country if they don't leave by plane. Cancelling doubt is difficult, but you must reveal the strengths of your arguments to counteract their doubts. Let's say that someone wanted to break off a relationship with you. You give them reasons to feel secured. Let them know why your love is strong. Talk out the situation calmly then build up whatever is lacking.

I must be a warrior in every aspect. Doubt is a weakness or fear in some such. It is my duty to cut off what has been debilitated and fill that void with encouragement.

Day 19

SEARCH THE DEEPEST DEPTHS or your inner being and somewhere amongst that shallow grave, you will realize that a living soul exists! Somewhere beyond your flesh is an inner man. That inner man is awaiting to be quicken, shook, and motivated. Some people never know what was instilled into them until they are compelled to do so. I never realize the hidden talents in me until I am forced to discover them. If I would have never been isolated from society, I would have never known of that hidden energy and strength. The reason I am able to do the things I do is because of an awakening of the inner man inside of me.

It will give me new life when I unravel my vitality.

Day 20

PLAY YOUR CARDS the way they are dealt! Life isn't always peachy. At times we win and sometimes we lose. However, we must abide by the rules and work with what we have. Taking risks play a major part in everyday living. Yet, if we are not in compliance, we will surely lose. We must fall in suit. As long as we are in order, we have a higher chance to win.

Today, I will learn how to utilize the hand that my life deals me.

Day 21

TO EACH HIS OWN! No matter whether you are male or female, you prefer to do things your way. What may work for you may not work for anybody else and vice versa. So who's to say that another person's actions or words are wrong? If it is right to them, it doesn't matter if it's wrong to you. To each his own goes right along with the saying "live and let live!"

I know that everybody has their own preferences.

Day 22

BE VERY SKEPTICAL of the games that people play with you. Also be aware of the jokes that they crack! Everybody's intentions are not amicable. They are characters posing to be friendly behind their gestures and hidden plans. Be aware of the jokes they crack. Some people pretend to be joking when they are really testing your reactions. They want to see how far they can take you. Also, watch the games they allegedly play with you. They are really seeing how much nonsense that you will accept from them.

It is okay to play harmless games and crack harmless jokes. However, if these games or jokes affect me in the long run, I will not entertain them.

ଔ୫୦ଔ

Day 23

EVERY TEST IS A TESTIMONY and all the mess is a message! Everything that we go through was designed to edify us. Just like before we were allowed to legally drive, we must first earn a permit by taking a test. Before we can graduate from school, we must pass all the tests that are given. Life is the same as school or college in a way. When we are faced with challenges, we have to pass the test of trials and tribulations in order to get ahead. Some people wonder why the same things happens to them repeatedly. It's because they have not passed the test in order to become an overcomer. For instance, let's just say that in every relationship you have had with the opposite sex, that person somehow cheated on you. That's because it's something in you that allows every person to feel that they can do these unruly things to you. Maybe it's because you told them about your past friends that cheated on you, so now this current person sees that you will accept it to a certain degree. Maybe they sense the vulnerability, gullibility, insecurity, desperateness, or they just know that you "need" someone to cling your heart on to. (Church people have this problem a lot because of their beliefs.) Whatever the case may be, we must pass the tests and endure all the mess and foolishness for a testimony to others. Your circumstances and situations talk to you at times and you don't even realize it.

I understand that messages are not always verbal. They speak through the mess that I go through. I know that I don't have to ace every test, but it is a necessity that I do pass the test.

Day 24

VISION DEMANDS CHANGE by its nature! This particular vision versus eye sight vision are two different things. A vision can be unusual. It could be like a super natural perception or a mental image produced by the imagination. A vision is something like a dream but it is more catered, planned and thought out more. In order for a vision to manifest, a change must occur. Perhaps, you have a vision of beginning your own company. You must go through the proper steps before it can show. That includes switching up your daily routines, investing irregular time, and dealing with people and things that you are not accustomed to.

When I have foresight, I must tackle it with all due diligence!

ꕥ

Day 25

YOUR PASSION has to be more powerful than the opposition to those around you! Have you ever noticed when people are losing in a game, sometimes they come back and win it all? I have seen people down in a card game by several points then they come back and win! In basketball and football they have a common saying, "The game is not over until the clock hits zero!" Do you know why that is? People's adrenaline and mindframe runs a thousand miles per hour when they are down. Their drive is more meaningful than the person that is winning. People that are close to victory tend to get relaxed and big-headed. While on the other hand, desperate causes for desperate measures. Before you know it the person getting defeated comes back and snatches the banner of victory from the leader's hand. That's how our drive has to be in real life to reach our achievement. Consistency and persistence play miraculous parts in the end.

It's true that some people fight better and more aggressively when their back is against the wall.

Day 26

WHAT YOU REALLY ARE will speak so loudly, that what you claim you are will not be heard! Have you ever heard that actions speak louder than words? That's because it does. So many people of this modern world claim to be this particular way but when it comes down to it their proclamation is irrelevant or supercilious to their theory. I know a man that has so much enthusiasm when he speaks that he could probably make a dead man get hype, but when it's all said and done, his actions are completely different from any word that he spoke. Lies become unraveled and his true motive behind the words are exposed. Personally, I'm allergic to these type of people. Beware or they will set you up for failure. If they are a coward acting like a villain, it will show!

I will focus more on who people are than what they claim to be.

Day 27

A FAIR EXCHANGE is not robbery! Some people want more than what is required or they want to get ahead by getting over on the next person. Rarely do people want to see eye to eye or be equals. Fairness is to be even and leveled.

I don't have to win all the time. It's is okay to have a tie.

Day 28

GOD DOES NOT want us to work for him. God wants us to work with him! Sometimes we put too much of a burden on ourselves. We take up an exceedingly amount of work or we want all the glory for a specific task. Instead of teaming up with the almighty we prefer to branch out on our own not knowing that God desires to be partners with us. Think about it. God can get done what he wants done without us. That's why companies fire their best workers at times. Even though their best workers invest all their time, effort, and maybe even sacrificed for the company or got the company ahead, they will still fire them because it's always someone out there that can do the same thing that they can do and probably do it better. So, in working with the creator we can get more accomplished as opposed to working at our own speed, our way, and with our attitude. We cannot go wrong when we work as a friend instead of a servant.

I know that they say "two heads are better than one" but working the God head is better than one million.

Day 29

YOU FIRST MUST ESTABLISH what you want to do and begin to do it before that need can be met! No one should just jump up and begin doing something and not be aware of what they are doing. That's like answering a question without knowing what the actual question is. Before every great project is finished a plan or thought has to be mastered first before it transpires. Once it has been conceived, then you can begin to energetically work towards the steps to apprehend the manifestation stages.

There are 3 steps to meeting my requirements. First, is the initiation or startup of what needs to take place. Second, is the mobility or movement to properly handling the necessities. Third, is executing the ending point so I can tell myself "job well done!"

Day 30

EVERYTHING DOESN'T ALWAYS go accordingly as planned! Many times I have had things thought out that didn't happen as I had planned. I'm pretty sure that we all have gone through this occasionally. Most of us don't have foresight so our expectations are not definite. To the contrary, even clairvoyance is not always one hundred percent accurate. Things tend to fail. That's why it is always wise to have a backup plan, be willing to abort the task or accept the best out of the situation, even if it's less than assumed.

I can't get caught up in a plan so much that it gets me down if it goes away. Every plan is not mandatory to succeed. If one plan flops then I must move to the next.

Day 31

WHEN LIFE deals you lemons, make lemonade! Some circumstances are going to seem sour or try it's best to make you bitter. No matter how the negativity or down fall occurs it is your responsibility to churn it. A lemon is very bitter if you decided to taste it after freshly peeling it; but if you squeeze the juice out of the lemon then add it to a cup with ice and shake it with sugar, you will have a sweet beverage. That is similar to the fundamentals of life. If you happen to lose your job, squeeze in every interview that you can find until you get another gig. If you are sick, do whatever it takes to cope with your illness. If a death occurs to a relative or friend let them live on through the sweet memories you cherish.

When life is bitter see what you can stir up to make it sweet.

Day 32

NEVER LET your left hand know what your right hand is doing! Have anybody ever side stepped you with a deal that you told them about? Or how about back doored you with some information that you thought was just between you two? Everyday people rush to outbeat someone else with the knowledge that they attained from the person that they are attempting to beat out. Swindling has no loyalty. There will always be people that go behind your back to either bite, be two faced, or short stop you. So never reveal what is deeply mourned for.

To avoid scandals, I will make sure that my business is situated before I speak on it.

Day 33

POTENTIAL is who you really are... the energy capacity and untapped power trapped inside of you! Inside of everybody, there is a stored power. Some of us do not realize it because we have never surfed the area. I never knew that I could write a book until I was compelled to do so. One day I was locked inside of a room with nothing else to do. I was bored out of my mind but couldn't sleep any longer. So, I told myself instead of reading all these books that I have already read, I'm going to attempt to write a book of my own and get paid for it. So, I began writing and the beginning sounded good to me. I continued writing than realized that I am a very great novelist. Every last one of us have our own repertoire. Yours may differ from mine and vice versa. We each have a gift that has to surface.

Today I will explore my undiscovered potential!

Day 34

DEAD FOLKS DON'T TALK! Show affection while and when you can. People can't hear "I love you" when they are incoherent or dead and gone. They cannot smell nor see the flowers you put on their graves. Embrace people now while you still have a chance. Don't wait until it's too late and you live to regret it. Holding grudges is folly on your behalf. When you forgive, you don't forgive for the sake of the person that wronged you but you forgive so that you won't have to live with resentment. You forgive so that anger won't build up and you end up catching a bad attitude or feeling at the thought of that person.

Enjoy the company of people before it's too late.

Day 35

THE ONLY THING WORSE than not thinking at all is thinking too much! Of course, when we don't think things out, we end up making foolish actions. There is one way that's more terrible than not thinking; and that is over thinking on a situation or person. When we over think, we tend to hallucinate and see more than what's actually there. We say things to people that have no idea of what we are thinking about. We start checking for stuff that is non-existent. Worst of all, we carry out in ways that are irrational and irrelevant.

I will see things for what they really are.

Day 36

I'D RATHER BE SMOOTH because being slick gets you in trouble! I was once talking to one of my childhood friends. She happened to ask me what was I doing at the time. I replied, "Truthfully, trying to snag me a female." Then I asked, "Do you have any advice?" I assumed since she was a woman herself and a lesbian that she would for sure know how to coat a lady friend. To my knowledge, she did just that. She said all I have to do is be smooth. I thought about it for a while then I came to conclusion what "smooth" means. Smooth means to be leveled, as in level headed. It means to not have wrinkles, flaws, or faults. Basically, she was telling me when it gets down to the nitty gritty, not to be blameless. Henceforth, she was right. Not only did I captivate the attention of a woman but I captured several. Usually, I would have tried to be slick in my younger days. Being slick only gets you so far until the people actually realize the slippery path that you created. Being slick means you have to cover up lies, be sneaky, untrustworthy, messy, and develop an image. In the end, no one will want to deal with you.

No longer will I be rough around the edges. My thoughts, actions, words, and intentions will be accountable and forever pleasing.

Day 37

IT IS NOT YOUR DUTY to be tolerant, it is your privilege! Do you know that some people think that you are supposed to accept their endeavors and attributes just because it is who they are? Well, what I am saying is that accepting anything from anybody is not mandatory; but it is your own choice and free will.

I do not have to tolerant anything. If I do, people ought to be honored.

Day 38

NIP IT IN THE BUD! The longer a problem occurs the harder it is to stop. That's why it is wise to end it as soon as it begins. Once a problem grows, it develops strength and it is difficult to root them up. It can be similar to dealing with troubling people. The first time that they do something you don't like, bring it to their attention. If it carries on, you will only bite your tongue more and more. This creates an avenue for a troubling person to establish a habit of mishandling you.

I will stop a person in their tracks before they get comfortable annoying me. I will cut the problems of circumstances and situations off before it gets out of control.

ᴓᴓᴓᴓ

Day 39

IF YOU FIND YOUR PURPOSE, you will find your prosperity! When we discover our reasoning for living riches will surely come to us abundantly. Whether it be inner or outer riches. The reason for this is because when we connect naturally, instead of dreading the work that we do, our talent will be so endowed that everyone around us will see that we are the best person for our position. Things line up perfectly when we are intact with what we were design to be. That's why a mechanic should do mechanical work. A mechanic would struggle with being a chef.

I will search and find what I was born to do because I know I will progress in that calling.

Day 40

PEOPLE WHO ARE SUCCESSFUL are like tea bags. When they get in hot water, they make tea! Have you ever heard the saying "when people throw salt on you, use it for seasoning?" Everything that is unruly and meant to hold you down should be that very thing you use to benefit from. I once read in the bible where it says "redeem the time." That means to make the best of every situation that we get into whether it is good or bad. If we get a scar on our face we should wear it proudly. It should be as a token that you survived a war wound. If you look on the bright side, most people probably would not be alive if they had experienced what you have been through.

I know that the greatest people in life will always come out on top, no matter how much dirt is thrown on them and no matter how bad of a situation they are in.

Day 41

HARMONY IS BASED ON an understanding of the forces constituting one's environment in a spirit of poise! Harmony is peace, rhythm, or tone in the functioning of your life. Since most individual's environment governs their feelings and how they conduct themselves, we must understand what controls the mass majority's behavior. Then we can go from there to balance out our inner peace.

I know that no matter what environment I am in, it is a spirit working in accord with one mind and one judgement. In order for me to keep the brotherhood, it must find a way to sustain tranquility.

Day 42

THERE ARE SOME GOOD PEOPLE in your life that are bad for you! I have met some pretty cool people in my life. However, it seems like every time they come around, it's always trouble of some sort. Now don't get me wrong, they are fun to hang with. They are always making me smile. They are very respectful. Yet, somehow they allow and attract negative energy. It's like they are a magnet for downfalls and mishaps. Truthfully, I don't think that they try to make these things happen. Perhaps they even try to prevent sadness. Nevertheless, with them, failure never fails.

I know that I could love someone with all my heart, but if they are an attraction for mischief, I must avoid them.

Day 43

EXPERIENCE is the best teacher! Sometimes you can tell people what to do and what not to do about a hundred times and they still will not get the lesson. You can show someone how to do something the best way that you know how and they will not understand the matter. However, when they do it themselves or go through the circumstances for themselves, only then will they be taught.

I can talk to people until I am black and blue in the face. I can show somebody how to do something until my fingers hurt. Some people will not get it until they have messed up and learned by experience.

Day 44

WHEN WE KNOW BETTER, we ought to do better! Time after time we repeat the same tragedies and ramifications because we don't evolve. Many of us know what to do but for some reason we just don't do it. I don't know if it's just because we are hard-headed, stubborn, or just plain rebellious. Whatever the case may be, we will never get the best until we start performing, talking, walking, and being the best version of ourselves. Not doing what you know that you are supposed to do is like taking a test and deliberately putting the wrong answers down.

I will not be a fool. When I learn what to do, I will apply. If I know something is not for me to do, I will avoid it.

Day 45

ONLY IF I KNEW THEN what I know now! I would have never made the mistakes that I did as a child if I had the information that I have now. I would have been so wise, invincible, and maybe even a millionaire if I was as smart as I am now in my younger days. Perhaps, I would have avoided some of the relationships I had. I would have invented many items, gone off to college, and saved more money. I probably would have never smoked a cigarette. I would have exercised a lot and I most definitely would have stopped a lot of bad things from happening.

I can't beat myself up over what I didn't know way back then. The only thing I can do now is think of the future so I won't have to repeat this quote again.

Day 46

IT IS BEST to already be ready. If you are already ready when it is time to be ready, you don't have to get ready! My sister once told me "If I'm on time, then I am late." I never understood that saying until today. What she meant was that if I am on time for a job, show, or performance, then I am behind others that got there early. I had no time for preparation or to just to take a breather. That's just like when it's time to make a move. Some will lose interest in your hesitation and procrastination.

I will not put things off to the last minute. I will always be ahead of schedule.

Day 47

KEEP ON KEEPING ON! Don't let anyone keep you from moving forward. It is your most precious joy to be mobile. No matter how many downfalls you have had or no matter how rough your excursion may seem, you must not give anybody the satisfaction of seeing you at a standstill.

By all means necessary, I must continue to strive. Moving up or going forward is my only option. Turning backwards or going down is a negative.

Day 48

LIVE IN THE MOMENT! We are not always sure of what the next minute or second may bring. In the twinkle of an eye, I have seen uprisings and upsets. You cannot get certain things back. You cannot relive the moments that have already passed, so enjoy them while they are there.

I will live for what is going on right now at this very moment.

Day 49

SOME PEOPLE HAVE what is called misplaced anger! They tend to taunt, annoy, aggravate or direct their indignation towards the wrong individual. They may be mad at their parents because of stress and peer pressure. They may raise their voice at their children or spouse because of what happened at their job. Perhaps, they bring problems from to work from home or vice versa.

I will not take my anger issues out on innocent people.

Day 50

SPEAK YOUR MIND! Don't let too much build up until the point where you will explode. Sometimes, holding back your words will make you regret forever what you didn't say. At the right place, at the right time, with the right line, you can save a life, gain prosperity, and even set yourself up for a great position. However, not speaking up at the right time can cause you to hate yourself or even have people running over you. I must also be aware to the reversal of every speaking. Talking too much can ruin friendships and relationships. You must weigh out what to say and what not to say. Timing is everything.

When I speak my mind, it relieves stress and won't destroy me on the inside.

Day 51

THE BEST GAME IS NO GAME. Be yourself! It amazes me how people try to be who they are not. Charlatans is what I call them. Pretending to be someone out of a movie, rap song, or someone that they have seen in their lives before. They are always telling people what they think they want to hear. People, it is easier to be yourself. Learn how to feel comfortable in your own skin. It is not nice always going around deceiving people and trying to play their mind with games.

It is time out for games. Keeping it real and genuine is the best thing going.

Day 52

YOU CAN FOOL some of the people some of the time, but you can't fool all of the people all of the time! A lot of people are very crafty at fooling others. All of their lives they succeeded in mastering the art of deception. Wheedling has become a part of their behavior and character. Almost everybody is tricked by their hidden talents. However, some people somewhere have already seen their kind and or their trade before. People have built an iron cloud against their tactics and see them before they get there.

Even if you are good at bamboozling, nine times out of ten you will get recognized.

Day 53

THOSE WITH A DEFINITE CHIEF aim demand respect and attention at all times! Nobody wants to be around a person that rarely has any certainty. People like people that know what they are doing and where they are going. When you are not indecisive but exalting and can prove progression through your work, you will be honored, praised, and others will be very attentive to you.The reason why the cameras are always on the superstars is because they have been shown to hit the bull's eye on their target. Meaning they are successful or have once touched the realm of prosperity.

When I know without a shadow of doubt what I am doing and where I am going in life people will subconsciously be submissive and always keep their eyes on me.

Day 54

EVERY CHAMPION does not win every round, but if he perseveres, he wins the match! Just because you happen to lose does not mean that you are not a champion. That lost was to inform you of something that you must learn to be aware of. Some boxers may lose every round, until they knock their opponent out in the tenth or twelfth round. Muhammed Ali is a perfect example. It takes time and perhaps suffering to peep out your opponents.

No matter what goes on, I must preserve my strength, energy, and grand act until the perfect timing to get back up and win again.

ꕥ

Day 55

NEVER UNDERESTIMATE ANYBODY! It will be your first and worst mistake by underestimating any person. Just because a person appears to be weak in a certain area does not necessarily mean it's true. Some people pretend to be debilitated so that you can test them. Some people play stupid to throw you off your guard. Others seem too naive to see how smart you really are. I once asked a person that if you had a politician, a doctor, lawyer, scientist, genius, professor, pimp, prostitute, and a naive person in the same room, who would be the craftiest person in the room? Believe it or not, the guy that answered the question got it right. The craftiest person in the room would be the naive person. First of all, how did the naive person get in the room with all of those well trained people anyway? They must be so uppity that they don't pay him any mind while he sucks up all their talents, conversations, and ways. The naive person is not really naïve, but he pretends to be naive so that he is overlooked. So, by him being overlooked, he has a piece of every person in that room. They may think he does not know what is going on, but he has learned more from them that they could ever imagine.

Underestimating is a sure way to get sucker punched emotionally, physically, financially, spiritually, and mentally.

Day 56

PLANT SEEDS! Women are good at planting seeds. They are born to nurture. They easily have their male companion doing things that they want him to do; but at the same time have him thinking that's what he wants to do and even after he has said he will not do it. When you plant seeds you don't rush anything. Insinuate something here and there or make suggestions every now and then. Talk about the subject that you want to input into that person's head. Yes, sometimes they will decline it in the beginning so ease it onto them. The catch is not to be forceful or too demanding. Speak indirectly so they won't catch on.

I don't know for certainty when the seed will grow that I have planted. It may take weeks, months, or years. If I cultivate the seed, in due time it will be fruitful.

Day 57

WE ARE VICTIMS of our habits! Whether we know it or not, our habits destroy us. They tear us down or have us neglecting people or things that if it wasn't for our habits, we wouldn't normally do. There are bad habits such as over-eating and smoking. Then there are good habits like being polite and grateful. No matter if they are good or bad our habits still victimize us because it may not be good to carry out every act all the time or treating every person the same. My mom once told me if you practice doing something a hundred times, then you can break a habit.

I will consciously attempt to break a habit ninety-nine times, except on that hundredth time. I won't have to practice doing it because it would have naturally become a part of me.

Day 58

IT'S OKAY TO BE HAPPY, but I prefer to have joy! To be happy, something has to be happening. It may make you happy to go to the park, fair, or movies. Receiving gifts, good grades, compliments, or attention could make you happy. When all of those things fade away, you are not happy any more until the next time something makes you happy. You will be nonchalant, idle, or just going with the flow. However, joy is quite different from being happy. Absolutely nothing could be going on and you will just be jolly as a joyful person. In the midst of trouble, pain, and terrible people, you will still have joy. No one or nothing can take away joy.

Happiness is a very good factor, but from now on I will be a joyous person.

Day 59

PLAY YOUR CARDS the way they are dealt! Life isn't always peachy. At times we win and sometimes we lose. However, we must abide by the rules and work with what we have. Taking risk plays a major part in everyday living. Yet, if we are not in compliance, we will surely lose. We must fall in suit. As long as we are in order, we have a higher chance to win.

Today, I will learn how to utilize the hand that my life deals me.

Day 60

KINDNESS IS THE LANGUAGE the deaf can hear and the blind can see! Languages are merely a way of connecting with someone. A person does not necessarily have to be able to see or hear to perceive what type of person you are. It is easy to pick up on your spirit. Do you not think that Stevie Wonder knows when a person is being kind or mean to him? Or do you not believe that a deaf person can actually see your actions? People have senses and intuitions that can pick up on your demeanor like radars.

Be kind because you are always being weighed by your behavior whether you know it or not.

Day 61

THERE'S ALWAYS ROOM left to grow! No matter how old, young, discouraged, or stubborn you have become, it is never too late to start growing and developing. So many people nowadays are so stuck in their ways until it becomes annoying to others. We have fixed in our minds that it's okay. Just because we are accustomed to something does not necessarily mean it's for the best.

We have to come up out of ourselves and allow a certain type of expansion to form.

Day 62

EVERYONE SAYS that forgiveness is a wonderful idea. That is ... until it's time for them to forgive someone! Things sound good when it does not involve you. Some people dislike being humble or having to be the bigger person. Their pride just will not allow them to be noble. Having to forgive someone is being a sucker or fool to them. They feel less of a person by excusing a fault. They do not realize that forgiveness is a virtue and a blessing in disguise.

When I forgive someone, I don't forgive them so they can feel better about themselves. I forgive them so I won't have to live with the animosity, anguish, and bad thoughts about that person every time I see them or hear their name.

Day 63

BLOWING out other folk's candles won't make yours shine any brighter! Hating or throwing salt on somebody will not make you seem any greater than the next. It only makes you look like an informant or dirty mack. True enough, people may keep you around just for the information but only if you knew what they were thinking deep down inside ...

If I stop another person from shining or ruin their career. It doesn't make me any difference from who I already was.

Day 64

IF CHRIST IS KEPT OUTSIDE, there must be something wrong inside! A lot of people do not want to invite anybody into their house if it is dirty and that's the same way with inviting Christ into your hearts. It's something you want to keep without giving up or either something you were taught wrongly. Maybe it's a feeling that needs cleansing. No matter what the case is, you will never know the valuable things you are missing until Christ makes a visit.

I must filter out the filth and let Christ have his way with me.

Day 65

ONLY CHICKENS can lay around and be productive. A human can't! I don't know why people think that they can achieve significant things by doing nothing. It is just not going to happen. We have to move around and become a go-getter.

I am not that goose that laid the golden egg. So, if I want any type of success, gold, or money, I must put forth honest work.

Day 66

IT IS BETTER for your heart to have no words than for your words to have heart! Sometimes it is good not to say anything at all than to say something you really don't mean. Words should be spoken out of the heart. Don't talk just to talk in vain.

Often, I may not know what to say, which is good, as long as my silence is genuine.

Day 67

A TRUE TEST OF CHARACTER is being put on a pedestal and not looking down on others! It's amazing how you could be friends with a person and as soon as they get in a certain position or an amount of money, they change. After prosperity, they act stuck up, like they are better than you and like they never been down before. They forget where they came from, who their real friends are, and most of all they forget how to treat people. They feel some people are scum of the earth or inferior so they don't deserve anything.

Just because I am up in life, I do not have to act uppity. Just because I have excelled does not mean I have to turn my nose up at others.

Day 68

FAMILY is supposed to stick together no matter what! We are humans, so we tend to have fallouts and disagreements with relatives like non-family members. However, our hearts pump the same blood and we are supposed to forgive and get over the hurdles. No one is flawless so let's not be resentful, stubborn, and so hesitant to forgive. Family is bigger than money, cars, clothes, houses, friends, jobs, and problems.

Today I will begin making amends with my family and those who were like family in my life.

Day 69

THE ONLY WAY you know you will surely sink is if you feel that your problems are bigger than your God! Nothing is certain unless all hope is lost in it. When we give up and don't depend on the higher power, we are surely destined for disaster.

I will stand firm in my belief because I am a conqueror as well as an overcomer. That is only if I know that my God is a giant, he is mighty, and stronger than my problems and situations.

Day 70

THE SAME ACTIONS, you get the same results! If you do not like the outcomes you are getting then attempt a different approach. Switch up from what you are accustomed to. People are constantly doing the same thing over and over yet the aftermath is not satisfied. Do it from a different angle. This is the same way in relationships. We wonder why we are always ending up with the wrong person or why we don't have anyone in our life at all. My advice to you is re-evaluate the circumstances, then take a different stand for better results.

Today, I will seek out new ways until my outcomes are likeable.

Day 71

WE DON'T ALWAYS have to learn what to do and why we should do it. Most of the time, we have to learn what not to do and why we shouldn't do it! Do not assume that you always know everything. Sometimes, we are dormant to certain facts and consequences. I once was talking to a young lady and I was aggressive because that was my nature and surroundings at the time. I also cracked mean jokes on her. I didn't pay it too much attention because that's the way that I played and humored my homeboys. I figured that she and I would only laugh at my jokes and she would accept my aggressive behavior because I was a man. Unfortunately, I ended up hurting this woman several times. She told me that she was used to the way that I talked to her. However, she was not going to allow me to be degenerate to her. I didn't want to lose a very special friend so I had to learn that I couldn't talk to her as I talked to my homeboys because she was overly sensitive. I had to learn how to downplay my aggressiveness because she blew things out of proportion. Yet, other women understood me so I didn't think that I was causing them any harm.

No longer will I only focus on the do's. I will mainly focus on the do nots.

Day 72

IF YOU CAN'T SEE eye to eye, it's best to depart! Some people have zero understanding with certain individuals. If you are always having problems, difficulty, and bad feelings every time you encounter a person, it is best to avoid or leave the presence of that man or woman.

I must understand that everyone is not made to get along with everybody. If two people don't come to see things the same way, I will evacuate the premise to avoid further destruction.

Day 73

EVERYBODY PLAYS THE FOOL! Just because a person appears to not know a thing or two does not always assume that they are blind to the facts. A lot of people want to see how you are going to act or treat them if they really were ignorant of the situation. Some people just want to avoid trouble so they play fooled or unknowledgeable. A lot of people like to live in denial so they don't say anything. Most people play it off by acting as if they don't know what's going on. They may wait until they have you cornered in before they bring the subject up or they may just be letting the negativity or benefits build up until they have enough evidence to settle the score with you.

Whatever the case may be, just because I may think a person doesn't notice or know something does not always mean that they don't.

ઊ઱ઌ઼

Day 74

GET WHAT YOU CAN, while you can, for as long as you can! At times when assets and revenue are running like water, capture all that you can. Don't assume that it will be there the next day or next week. Get all that is available and store it for a rainy day. Stretch out the last little drops and drain every ounce of the valuable substance.

When things run out, it is over for me. There is no returning to the first state or nature as I may think.

Day 75

WHATEVER WE HAVE BROKEN, we can rebuild. Whatever we have destroyed we can re-make. Those things we have forgotten can be re-learned. What we have done can be undone only if we choose to undo them. Do you believe that things are forever lost? Some things may not ever be in the exact state or stage as before but you can make a duplicate.You can re-attempt until you succeed at what has failed even if it takes you forever recompensing or establishing a thing over. Even commitments can be revisited. People are quick to forget certain things so a reminder would be nice.

Renovation, innovation, and remodeling are some things that I must begin to do immediately.

Day 76

BE CAREFUL when you point a finger at someone because you will always have 3 of them pointing right back at you! Have you ever noticed that when you are pointing a finger towards any direction, 3 of your own fingers are pointing right back at you? That's the same way with other people also. If you are directing a finger at another human being, at least 3 other people are pointing one at you. It may not be pertaining to the reason I think, but they are aimed for their own purposes.

Whatever I do, I better believe that somebody is doing it to me or going to do it at some point. It may not be in the same form that I did it, but it will be manifested.

Day 77

A FRIEND THAT HELPS a friend in need is a friend indeed! A lot of people pretend to be friendly until it is time to aid and assist. When it's time to help, they cut their phone off, don't answer doors, get speechless, turn you down, act like they don't have it, or get quiet. A true friend will always be there regardless. No matter how difficult your situation is. They will help you even if it's just kind words, a shoulder to lean on, a hug, food, shelter, clothing, money, or a ride.

I will not allow people to pretend to be a friend to me when they really are not.

Day 78

YOUR ACTIONS will determine your success in life! What you do from this day forward will be proof of whether you become a failure or a success. So, monitor your every move and always think far in advance before you make a move.

My actions are very valuable and important. If I make the wrong moves, my outcome will be horrible. If I make the correct moves, I will be mighty proud.

Day 79

BE DILIGENT to control your emotions so that your judgment will not be clouded! People cannot think clearly when they are frustrated, furious, depressed or annoyed. Majority of the world's population think with their feelings instead of logically or rationally. That is why rage and other components of emotion have you far from seeing a vivid picture. Emotions and sensitivity is a sure way to underestimate, lose, stress, hallucinate, and not be susceptible. Judgment should be wise, just, honest, and totally unbiased. Anything other than that is not fair.

I must set my emotions aside so that I will not make choices that I will later regret. I shall not make unruly or unequal judgments.

ଔଔ

Day 80

FREEDOM IS NOT FREE! What is freedom? The dictionary describes it as not being imprisoned or enslaved. To be at liberty, costing nothing or not be under obligation. But who's to say that being able to do our own free will is freedom? No matter what you do or say, there will always be opposition. Whether you do good or bad someone will always have their opinion to voice against you. Just because you are not behind bars you still don't live freely. You have to do chores and pay bills. You still have rules and regulations to follow. You cannot do any and everything that you want to do or when you want to do it.

Everything has a price.

Day 81

UNDERSTANDING is the best thing! No matter how much wisdom and knowledge you obtain. If you don't have understanding then your information is in vain. The reason why people have so much confusion and animosity against each other is because they don't have an understanding of one another's ways and attitudes. If we understood why people do what they do or say what they say, then we can live a more peaceful life. Sometimes we take gestures and words out of content. We are misled by attitudes and facial expressions and begin to act out without trying to put their shoes on our feet. We have to learn how to view things in more than one angle.

Without understanding my wisdom, with knowledge and learning amounts to nothing.

Day 82

IF YOU FIX in your mind that your ability is limited to a given earning capacity, you will never earn more than that! You will hardly ever receive more than what you believe you are entitled to. A lot of people downplay themselves. They lose hope and confidence and thus they do not elevate. What you have in your mind is what you will get. If you think big then you will achieve highly. If you think peanuts and pennies, that is what you will have.

I have heard, "As man thinketh so is he." That is exactly true.

Day 83

YOU CAN CATCH A LOT more bees with honey than you can with vinegar! Have you ever noticed that you can get more accomplished with kind words than you can with angry ones? How about sweetness has more results than bitterness? That's because good ways are more convenient than bad ways, and righteousness overrules evil.

Cleaning up my actions will give me more success than my filthy ways.

Day 84

IF YOU REASON WITH SOMEONE, it is not giving in or accepting, it is simply reasoning! When you talk to a lot of people, instead of them trying to understand what you are saying, they are fixing in their head what they are going to say next while you are talking to them. A lot of people communication skills are their only comeback, reasoning has no foundation in their persona. They haven't realized that all the knowledge and information that they have is vain without understanding. Even the bible says with all your knowledge getting, get understanding. Understanding is the principle thing.

From now on, I don't only want to get my point across, but focus on the understanding of others as well.

Day 85

A SECRET ISN'T A SECRET if you tell it. Some people can't hold water which is why you can't confide in them. You may be looking for a confidant to get some things off your chest but the person that you want to entrust this information with is a blabber mouth. You can ruin relationships and friendships by running your mouth. Families have been destroyed by the flap of a tongue. We need to think before we speak. Everything is not meant to be told. If that person wanted other people to know what they told you they would have told them themsevles instead of telling you.

If somebody tells you something, as long as it is not going to cause harm to anyone or prevent tragedy from happening, please keep it to yourself.

Day 86

A PAIR OF LIPS can be fixed to say anything! People can say whatever they chose to say. Some things may have consequences behind them, but they can speak on it if they chose to. Just because somebody says something does not necessarily mean it's the truth. I have seen many people portraying to be a sheep but they are really a wolf seeking to devour you. Even if a person is proclaimed to be a nun, I will still take what they say into consideration. A lot of people say things just because it sounds good or it makes them look good. Some people say stuff merely to make you feel comfortable. I know people that lie and probably don't even realize it because they are so use to lying or they have begun to believe their own lies. I have been around pros, cons, masters of manipulation, and compulsive liars. The worst kind are icons and public figures such as politics, lawyers, prosecutors, preachers, and teachers that will tell you something but don't even believe what they told you themselves.

I cannot believe any and everything that comes out of someone's mouth.

Day 87

IT IS WHAT IT IS! Something people have to be is nonchalant, so that they won't get overly emotional or ruin some things. You are not always content with what is going on in your life or the people you are with, but you acknowledge that what is going to happen is going to happen anyway, and the people around you are going to always be who they are. To care less or be unbothered is a good way to handle some situations, problems, and people; but not all of them.

Sometimes I have to be in "whatever" mode.

Day 88

WHAT IT IS NOT, it will never be! We have to face the fact that some things will never happen. Some people will never change. Either we can deal with it, or we must improvise.

Trying to force things that were not meant to happen will leave me scared or with a burden.

Day 89

THERE ARE PEOPLE that are not physically locked up but they are still incarcerated in their mind, finances, social skills, emotions, and spirit! I have seen people in jail that are more in tune with reality and life than people that are not behind bars and wired fences. These convicts have a peace of mind and accept what is thrown at them by making the best out of their situations. They are not uptight, neither do they panic when nature's horrors advance unto them. On the other hand, I have seen people that are free to do what they want, pleased with the assets they have, and still these people are boxed in their own situations. The emotions have them confined and they only have a one track mind. When it comes to finances, they are blinded by the sunlight in order to make their currency flourish. The worst thing of all is that they believe in their own mind and that they don't have the time to get in tune with their spiritual life.

Instead of judging all inmates, I may need to attempt to learn something from a few of them.

Day 90

THOUSANDS HAVE SEARCHED yet failed to realize that the greatest treasure lies between two temples! People have traveled to Rome, Egypt, and other ancient places to dig in tunnels, check tombstones and deep dark constructions to unscramble this riddle. However, they still haven't constructed the stanza. Once they understand it, it will improve their lifestyles and the people around their lives. Yet, this day I will reveal to you the location of these mighty two temples. You don't need a shovel, chisel, nor a bull dozer to unravel it. If you take your fingers and rub it against the side of your head, you will massage the temple. Between those two temples is the greatest treasure on earth, which is your brain.

People look for money and gifts all the time to make us happy, but all we have to do is use our mind as a valuable treasure.

Day 91

WE MUST DELETE "trying" from our vocabulary, because "trying" carries doubt and fear! Instead of trying, we must step up to the plate and be bold. At the end of the day, it's either you do it or you don't do it. You either fail or succeed. There is no in between.

I must recognize that trying is an excuse.

Day 92

THE DARK CLOUDS OF LIFE look gloomy passing by, but know that they will one day pass and reveal sunshine! It is true that nothing lasts forever. All things must come to an end. No matter how obscure your situations and life seems to be. One day you will have joy.

Even though times may be hard on me now, I must withstand and make the best of things until light is shining towards my direction.

Day 93

A LOST OPPORTUNITY is a failed success! Every chance that we get to make something happen and ignore it, it could be ignorance on our own behalf. Success can come between a split-second decision because it comes close to almost never happening at all. When we let things slip out of our hands or get away from us, most times, we have been defeated and considered as failure. Even though this is not the case in some theories, it is in most.

I have to understand that sometimes opportunity only knocks once, so if I miss it then I lost out severely.

Day 94

IT'S JUST A MINOR SETBACK for a major comeback! Our mishaps, downfalls, and setbacks are something that we should use to recuperate and view the elements of the situation in another fashion. For darkness to be exposed, light must shine on your circumstances.When you fall off, make a comeback that's harder, stronger, and more divine than you ever have before. The ones that were happy about your downfalls will turn their smiles into frowns in an instant.

Minor breakage is nothing compared to a major build up. So, I must turn a negative into a more valuable positive.

Day 95

I HEAR, BUT I DON'T HEAR. I see, but I don't see. I know, but I don't know! Everything that we see, hear, or know is not supposed to be exposed. Some things are to kept confidential, quiet, or secretive. When we go around ear hustling we hear things that can affect us, confuse us, or mislead us. Therefore, we have to filter out conversations. Even some things that we see are not actually what we assume they are. The eyes can be deceptive. So, it is good to plot out the memory of things once seen. A lot of people like to be nosey until the point that they can't see or realize what's going on in their own life. Everything that you see is not beneficial. What you know can hunt you or hurt you. Sometimes, we have to un-know what we know. Some knowledge is too high to obtain. It is not good to believe you know everything.

I can see, hear, and know things, but at the same time not pay any attention to it.

Day 96

WATCH YOUR SURROUNDINGS before your surroundings surround you! If you are not careful and observant of your environment, atmosphere, and the company that you keep then those things can take you out unknowingly.

I will always pay attention to the people and things around me so that they cannot over power me.

Day 97

THE NUMBER ONE FEAR is fear of the unknown! A lot of people are afraid of spiders, snakes, and heights. Some believe that the number one fear of all people is the fear of death, fear of living in poverty, or fear of having bad health issues. Even though the above list of fears are common amongst people, they are not the number one fear. People fear what they don't know or what they are not aware of. Most people do not change because they fear what might happen or what might not happen. A lot of people are more frightened of living than they are of dying because they don't know what's ahead.

It is not always good to get comfortable with all people and situations, because once I become accustomed to certain things or people, I will not be prepared for what happens next.

Day 98

DON'T LET YOUR ENVIRONMENT, people around you, or situations define who you are! Your attributes and endeavors should be solely based on your goals, visions, and purposes for living. You cannot let anything or anybody predict your attitude or state of mind.

I know that people and situations are quick to get me down but I will not allow it.

Day 99

WE AS PEOPLE have to train others how to treat us! Don't assume that the average person automatically knows how you should be treated. You are unique and an ethereal human being. Most never encountered one such as your caliber. No matter how old or how young a person is, their position, race, nor gender does not establish their molding ability. Step up, speak up, and if one gets out of line then align them back up.

Get people to fall in suit.

Day 100

NEVER LET another person's words dictate your mood! Why are people so overly worried about what another person has to say about them? I'm more concerned with what my God thinks of me. I'm not too big on letting others words and thoughts get to me. They talked about Jesus Christ over 2000 years ago and his name still rings until this day.

It is true that sticks and stones can break my bones but words should not hurt me.

Day 101

BE WISE ENOUGH to learn from other's mistakes! It's a famous commercial that has been playing for decades. In the commercial you see a car run into a brick wall then you here a man say, "You can learn a lot from a dummy." That statement is so true. You can learn exactly what not to do from a dummy. However some of us see clues and get warnings from looking and listening at other individuals then we go and entangle ourselves with the same problems, thinking that we will not be affected like the next (drugs and alcohol are a major factor in this). Even though mistakes and defeat make us aware, let it now make us better.

A lot of us already know what to do. Now since we have that knowledge let's know the opposite.

ꕥ

Day 102

ANYTHING WORTH HAVING is worth working with or working for, and anything having is worth waiting for! Nothing worth having comes easy. It's a price to pay for everything and even to be with that significant other. Sacrifices are necessary. Compromises must be done. Meeting people half way is required. It may get hard, lonely, upsetting, and tiresome but the wait will be beneficial. Just remember that all work comes with labor but the payout will make you want to do it again.

I know that the easier things come the easier it goes. So, if I want something permanent then I must conserve and preserve.

Day 103

THE MAIN REASON why people disrespect you and don't take you seriously is because they know that there isn't consequences for not taking you seriously or disrespecting you! Maybe in your mind you are thinking of taking actions or making a statement against the ones that run over you or neglect you. Maybe you are the one that second guesses and change your mind. However, until people realize that there are repercussions for not taking you serious or disrespecting you they will do it forever, especially if you are the one that is supposed to be in charge.

I cannot always find good in everything that people say and do. I must realize some things are offensive. Giving the benefit of the doubt is futile.

Day 104

ONE MAN'S TRASH is another man's treasure! Somebody will always value the next thing a person more than you. Just because something doesn't fit right for you doesn't mean that it's not perfect for the next woman or man. Things that you throw away can become a high commodity to the next human. People that see you as insignificant will be very loving and meaningful to the next.

Everything and everybody is supremely valuable to someone else. I must never forget that.

Day 105

THERE ARE ONLY THREE types of people in this world: 1) The type that make things happen. 2.) The type that things happen to. 3.) The type that watch things happen.Things happen around us all day every day. It is inevitable whether it will be small or great, and at what times. No matter if you watch someone make money, they get the money from you, or you are the recipient of the money, somehow the transactions may be bad things happening to you all the time or you always see or notice bad things happening to others. Perhaps, you are the one dishing out the trouble. It still involves you. Something is going to always happen whether you like it or not. My advice is for you to decide which side you want to be on.

Find out what type of person you are than work to become the type that you desire to be.

Day 106

TEMPER GETS YOU into trouble and pride keeps you there! Hot headed people rarely make wise decisions. Yet, when they do get into trouble their temper won't let them make the sacrifices or gain the humility to recover. Pride is a terrible thing. Pride will have you struggling and not ask for help. Pride will have you hungry and turn down a gift of food.

When I learn to swallow my pride, only then I will began to climb out of the tunnels I have dug for myself.

Day 107

BY YIELDING TO TEMPTATION, one may lose in a moment what it took a lifetime to gain! Temptation is a clever but dangerous beast. Temptation can come in all sorts of ways and have many tactics. Temptation can be greed, lust, anger, giving up, or many other of varies things. Temptation has caused people to lose their spouses, jobs, kids, finances, and even their relationship with god. It only takes a second to subdue to temptation and come up short upon what it took forever to build.

Temptation will come, but I must resist it.

Day 108

A SMILE is an inexpensive way to improve your looks! People don't have to always buy clothes, jewelry, and cars to look good. Just a simple smile can make you look better than the average person. A smile brightens up a person's day and makes them feel warm and comfortable with you. It will also make you feel wonderful about yourself.

Smiles and laughs are very impressive to me.

Day 109

I'M NOT IN THIS WORLD ALONE, so I must get along! My main goal is to satisfy my loved ones. I grew to appreciate what they like and care for what they admire. The best way to get completely along with certain people is to be conveyed into their world. What you once didn't notice, you will become to realize it now or what you have never done before, you will become accustom to it.

I may not use to like doing certain things, being around particular people, or going to extreme places; However, I love it now for the simple fact that someone whom I like, likes it.

Day 110

TO SHOW TRUE AFFECTION is to bend over backwards! If you know anything about an acrobat or gymnast then you would know that it is very difficult to bend over backwards. To bend over backwards is basically something like the actor did in the matrix movie. However, If you truly love someone then you will go out of your way to make that person happy. You are willing to take the risk if that's what it takes to show your affection.

There shouldn't be a question asked once sincerity is shown and provided.

Day 111

ENOUGH IS ENOUGH! Some people just over do things at times. They don't know when the stopping point is. When you go pass the limits or boundaries that is a sure way to cause problems and stress. I have seen people even over do their jobs. It's okay to do your job but you don't have to be institutionalized.

I must realize that some things are just not caused for.

Day 112

WHEN YOU GET VIBES and chills that is a sure way to know that what you are facing or dealing with is the real deal! Sometimes vibes and chills are supernatural. It's like that gut feeling in your stomach or your intuition to warn you or to let you be aware of what's ahead. Vibes and chills is also confirmation, agreements, or disagreements. Vibes and chills can be good or bad.

From now on I will take heed to my chills and vibes.

Day 113

SHOOTING FOR THE CLOUDS is too low. Instead, aim higher and make the clouds your cushion just in case you fall! Almost everyone always say that the sky is the limit. I guess that is okay if you want to align with other's limitations. Personally, I like to exceed. I aim higher than the sky. If I happen to have a downfall or setback then the clouds will be where I land. In other words, if everyone else's target was to reach a hundred, I will aim for a thousand. If others seem to just want to work for the company one day, then I plan to own the company.

The next time people tell me that they are attempting to reach the sky, I will tell them that I'm aiming for the moon.

Day 114

WATCH the miraculous changes that occur when you begin to put God first! The best way for things to line up in our life is to seek the one that gave us life in the first place. When you place a higher power at the head of everything than you do, say, and think then doors suddenly begin to open that you never thought would open.

Miracles still do happen. I just have to let God be in charge before they do.

Day 115

PROSPERITY doesn't mean that tomorrow's need is met today, it means that today's need is met today! We have to live for the day that we are in because tomorrow isn't promised to anybody. I'd rather enjoy today peacefully instead of being stressed about tomorrow. To prosper is to succeed in what you need for that day. You cannot eat nor drink today for tomorrow.

I can't worry myself to death about tomorrow because tomorrow will take care of itself.

Day 116

SOMETIMES WE GET in our own way! At times, we literally stumble over ourselves mentally, socially, financially, and spiritually. We tend to jump the gun often saying and doing things that are uncaused for or unnecessary. We attempt to advance too quickly and end up getting lost in words, thoughts, feelings, or actions. Somebody may want to bless us with something but we end up over talking and talk ourselves out of the blessing.

I must realize that it is me blocking my own way at times.

Day 117

THE ONLY THING that has power over you is the thing that you allow to have power over you! Nothing can overtake you unless you entertained it or had some type of contact with it. We are in control of our own destiny. Even God the creator gives us choices to choose either right or wrong. We always have an escape route to get pass what's overwhelming.

I have to be strong and wise to gain authority over the matters in my life.

Day 118

EVEN SOLDIERS get wounded, but what makes a soldier a warrior is when he or she gets back up to fight again and win again! We will all encounter some type of setback and downfall. Pain is hard to miss out on all the days of our lives. But when these elements occur, we stand up when we get knocked down; keep going even when we feel we are out of strength; and continue to plan even if every other plan has failed. We must still believe although the way looks blurry. There is sunshine at the end of a dark tunnel.

I must realize that medals and awards come with warning. The fight should never be over. I will not give up or give in.

Day 119

GOOD AND BAD are not in the circumstances, but only in the mind of those that encounter it! Good and bad is all in how you view your situation. What's bad to you may not be the same to the next person. If there wasn't a such thing as good, there would be no bad and vice versa.

We must randomly look at things and people from different angles.

Day 120

A LARGE PART of the gift of cultivation is the ability to see potential in what others view as wasteland! There are many empty fields or lots where people dump their trash at. To the average eye they may not even glance at the site. To them it is clutter or filth. However, one man or woman may pass that same dump site or vacant fields and see opportunities to build businesses over the wasteland or field. They can get the land for cheap since not too many will want to purchase the land. Another person may turn that same investment into a multi-million-dollar company.

I should open my eyes wider to see what's there in any property, business, or person.

Day 121

THE GREATEST POINT of failure is when you are close to victory! Havoc, confusion, chaos, and disappointments normally happen to get your eyes off of the blessings or miracles that are suddenly approaching you. It is quicker to lose your cool when you know you deserve better.

While the enemy is working over here you better believe that God is working somewhere else.

Day 122

YOU WILL KNOW without a shadow of doubt when you find your soulmate! Surely a person that goes out of the way for you is truly a person that cares of you. To sacrifice and humiliate one's self for another's pleasure is a token of passion.

I must not overlook another person's actions towards me. If they are willing to lower them self to life me up then that is the one for me.

Day 123

SMALL MINDS talk about people. Average minds talk about events. Great minds talk about ideas! People are always talking about other people. Some do it because they don't have anything to do or they are either jealous, envious, or have hatred towards the individuals. People that stay focus on speaking on another person hardly ever prosper. It is okay to speak on events to stay in tune with what's going on around you. This is what the ordinary person does. Whether they benefit from the event or not, they have to have an input on it. Great minds get things done whether it's functions, business, relationships, inventions, growth, development, friendships, etc. Great minds talk about uprisings and downfalls and how to avoid setbacks, kinks, leaks, and how to fix glitches. Great minds are always attempting to make things and people better.

I have to figure out what kind of mind I have. I can rearrange it to the kind of mind that I need if I want to.

Day 124

IT'S A PROCESS to progress! We must all go through some kind of courses, challenges, channels, or methods to get where we need to go. A lot of us get discouraged once we begin facing situations and circumstances that we must handle. Yet, we shouldn't worry because the changes are necessary.

I must follow the correct steps or chain of command before I am fully advanced.

Day 125

TENSION IS FORMED when negative things happen or bitter and angry words are released! If you ever wondered why it is so hostile in your household or people had resentment against you, maybe you need to realize the words that you speak and the things that you do. Kind words will make your living peaceful and your home sweet, but cursing and fussing will create problems.

Words are very powerful, so I know I must monitor my language and actions.

Day 126

THERE IS ONE WAY to overcome being a slave and that is by steady and persistent growth in inward knowledge! You can become a slave to society by not knowing what's going on around you. Ignorance is not acceptable. We must always continue to advance and be aware of uprisings so we won't end up on the shorter end of the stick.

We must know our rights whether it's lawful, constitutional, rules and regulations in our cities, schools, neighborhoods, or jobs.

Day 127

DESTINY DEMANDS DILIGENCE! You have to be energetic and give it your all if you want to meet your destiny. That means waking up early or going to sleep late. You may miss meals or quality time with people. Destiny is in high demand so we must supply it with our strength and all of our mind and soul.

You must go out there and muscle your way. Be hype to fulfill your destiny.

Day 128

YOU WILL BE BLESSED by saying yes to what is in accordance with your vision and no to anything else! How rare do we say yes or no just to get along with others or to please them? The words we speak may not feel good but it should always line up with our dreams, goals, and visions.

The only thing that I will approve is what aligns with what I have going on in life.

Day 129

LOYALTY is not just a word. It is a lifestyle! Nowadays, a lot of people aren't loyal to the ideas and feelings of others. Self-gain, self-interest, and fabrication have become an epidemic. People say words and don't mean what they say. They might claim what they are going to do and never do it. They may even say they aren't going to do a thing and then end up doing that very thing they said they wouldn't do.

If I deal with a person, they must be loyal. I will not accept faithless or dishonest people unless they are going to be loyal.

Day 130

LEARN TO LEARN! A lot of people are stuck in their ways. They Think that they know everything. Their mind has been closed to learning. We must be willing to learn.

I must develop a skill to learn.

Day 131

EVERYTHING has an advantage and disadvantage to it! If you look deep enough into anything, it has a benefit or handicap in it. The most favorite thing you love has a weakness and a strength in it.

From now on, I will weigh out my options.

Day 132

WE HAVE TO LOOK past what we want to get what we need! What we want at times has more pleasure in it than the things we actually need. Needs may come with sacrifices, labor, or having to tone yourself down. What we want is enjoyable and nice things that appeal to the eyes. However, what we want is a blindfold to what we truly need.

I can't let my wants become a blindfold to what is necessary.

Day 133

STICK TO THE SCRIPT! Our lives are already written out in the way that it is going to go. Just like we have plans, dreams, and goals, when things are already figured out we should go accordingly as the script was engraved. If we get off track or detour off course then things will begin to fall apart and people will back away.

I will not deviate but I will be cohesive to the plan.

Day 134

WE MUST REMAIN solid like a rock and rooted like a tree! To stand your ground is to not be uprooted or moved by anything. We cannot let problems or people weaken us. We must be strict in our beliefs and characters. Do not be easily persuaded, convinced, or deceived.

I will be strong in all my ways and in my mind. I will not let anything or anyone debilitate me.

Day 135

THERE IS A DIFFERENCE between being a woman, a lady, and a girl! A girl is an adolescent who hasn't faced the trials and tribulations of the world. A girl does not have wisdom and understanding such as an elder. She is naive and vulnerable. A lady is one whom may claim to be grown because she has a child, house, job, or car. She doesn't know that being grown doesn't necessarily make you mature. Maturity is the next level that a lady must meet. A lady prefers to play games and be hard on people simply because she believe she can. She has a lot to learn. A woman has mastered the art of living. She knows when to do something and how to do it in fashion. A woman also knows what to do to complicate problems and situations even further. She is virtuous and loyal. She is also level headed and open minded.

I will find out what type of person I am dealing with, then I will proceed further.

Day 136

WEATHER the storm! When problems come your way, you must blend in with them. That means to make preparation and not let them get the best of you. Whatever you encounter, make sure you get through it safely and survive.

I will condition myself for whatever I face.

Day 137

YOU HAVE NEVER walked in my shoes! You are not me and I am not you. You may have faced similar things that someone else has faced but you didn't encounter those exact same things. Therefore, you can't judge how another person acts.

My pain is pain and my joy is joy. My joy or pain isn't anybody elses.

Day 138

IT'S GOOD TO VENT for the right cause! We shouldn't keep a lot of tension bottled up because sooner or later it will explode. Venting doesn't necessarily mean nagging or bragging. Venting is getting things off your chest or out of your tension before it builds up.

To avoid stress, depression, anxiety, and disappointments I will vent in *order to be relieved.*

Day 139

YOU HAVE TO LOVE yourself before you are able to love somebody else! You cannot truly love another person without loving who you are yourself. If you think you love someone without loving yourself it is not true love. If you will hurt yourself then you will hurt others by hurting yourself or doing things that show lack of care for yourself such as drugs, alcohol, prostitution, lying, cheating, gang-banging, etc.

I will love myself genuinely.

Day 140

ONLY the strongest survive! Passive people that need to be pacified hardly ever survive the storms of life. Trials and tribulations will destroy the weak minded and free hearted. Strong willed minded people are overcomers. They will get over the hurdles of life and make it through the mazes. When tests come, the strong will knock them down.

I must have strength in all my ways.

Day 141

A HEART OF GOLD is hard to get and hard to hold! A heart of gold is pure, unique, and blameless. Not everyone can contain a heart of gold. It is hard to get a heart that is good in this cold and harsh world. If you have a heart of gold then people, problems, and situations may make you want to change your golden ways.

I will hold on to what I have and develop what I need.

Day 142

LEARN TO LISTEN more than you speak! Have you ever heard people say that we have two ears but only one mouth so we should hear as twice as we speak? Well, that proverb is true. I once worked for a major car dealership. By me being fresh on the scene I figured that I could talk people into buying a car since I felt I was a smooth talker. Whenever a customer approached me I would take them to a car or truck and tell them how cool the vehicle was, how much gas it can save or how good they would look in it. Unfortunately, I didn't sell a lot of cars that way. One day my manager called me to talk to me. He told me that he had been observing me. He told me that the key to selling cars is not talking the person into buying a car but listening to what they want. After I took his advice I began to meet the customers with their needs. I began listening to what they wanted and selling them what they desired instead of attempting to talk them into what they didn't want.

If I want a healthy relationship, friendship, or work style, I must listen to understand and not do all the talking.

Day 143

THERE IS NO VICTORY unless there is a battle! To overcome evil, struggles, strong holds, sorrow, bad mind battles, pride, judgement, un-forgiveness, impatience, hatred, fears, jealousy, and division then it must be a war. The more opposition resists you, persist until you triumph.

Victory is a wonderful thing but I must put up a fight.

Day 144

IF YOU WANT TO RUN something or be somebody that's important then that means you have to be willing to accept everything that comes with the territory! People want to have glory and be in the spot light but don't want to deal with the strings attached to it. Being in authority has consequences and responsibilities like none other.

I must pay the fee to get above.

Day 145

DON'T LIVE TO EAT but eat to live! Too much of anything is bad for you. When people live to eat they become lazy, overweight, have difficulties with moving, and have all sorts of health problems. Everything they see or think of they want to eat. Eating is like a hobby or craft to them. Most times you don't be hungry. It can be your mind telling you that you are. When you only live to eat you feel lighter so you are able to move swifter. Your system feels better and food does not control you because your mind is stronger than a substance.

I will not over eat. I know now that I can survive off of small portions.

Day 146

THERE IS NO SUCH THING as a silly question. The only senseless question is the one you didn't ask! Don't let anyone prevent you from learning or having knowledge of a situation. Knowledge is a key and very valuable to your achievements. Just because you may know something doesn't mean that the next person should automatically know the same and vice versa. So no one should turn a person's question down and label it stupid.

I will ask all the questions that I need to know.

Day 147

I MUST GO THROUGH all that I'm going through to get where I'm going to! Sometimes we cannot help what is in front of us. Traveling to our destiny is like riding down a highway with pot holes, debris, and animals jumping out in front of you. We may have to zig and zag to make it where we need to go. Our destiny may even be long and tiring, but we must go that direction and encounter the people along the road.

I will go through to get to.

Day 148

ALWAYS THINK before you speak! No man or woman should just randomly blurt things out. Your first thought isn't always accurate. We should analyze the things we are going to say before we say them. We should know the effect that our words will have.

It is good to be a quick thinker but a quick speaker is not for me.

Day 149

FLIP THE SCRIPT! If you don't like the way things are going or how people are acting then make a change in accordance of how you are content with them. If someone says a something that you disagree with then turn the entire conversation around to fit your way. Perhaps you can turn the circumstances from off you and onto them.

From now on, I will turn things around and make positive changes.

Day 150

FAITH CANCELS DOUBT but doubt cancels faith! If you ever had any type of lack of confidence, distrust or things that are just not clear to you, you can boost your confidence up and terminate your disbelief with assurance of hope that you will pull through. Faith will take away uncertainty. On the other hand, if you don't believe in anything then 9 times out of 10 it may not happen. Your mind will waver with doubt, your discernment will be uneased, you will be indecisive, and suspicious.

One thing will always over rule the other, I have to choose which one will lead. I prefer to keep the faith.

Day 151

ONLY SPEAK when you are spoken to! The best way to keep down confusion and not say what's appropriate is to remain silent. We should let others lead the conversation first just to see where their mind frame is at. We don't want to be ashamed by stepping out of line for saying something until nobody has any idea of what we are talking about.

I will always speak when it is my turn.

Day 152

ANYTHING that doesn't kill me only makes me better! All kinds of challenges and forces enter into our daily worlds. If whatever we face does not kill us then we should use that as a substance to grow and develop into a better person.

If whatever I encounter does not destroy me permanently then I will become greater.

Day 153

REGARDLESS, always do what is necessary! No matter the consequences do what is reliable. Even if people don't like the choice you made, still do what's appropriate.

It is mandatory for me to do what it necessary.

Day 154

NOBODY IS PERFECT, but you can find somebody that is perfect for you! Everybody has flaws. Real life and real people are not fairytale. A lot of people are single today because they have dreamed and made up a perfect person in their mind. However, they may find a high percentage towards perfect but they will never find someone who is completely impeccable. On the other hand, you can meet someone that meets your requirements, needs, and desires. Someone can be that special one for you and satisfy you.

I am not perfect and neither will my spouse be.

Day 155

THINGS GET WORSE before they get better at times! When we are expecting good things to come into our lives we want them to happen either speedily or suddenly especially when we are already enduring hard times. But little do we know, situations go from bad to worse in a split second. So once all the rotten and worse things has passed us by it has no choice but to get better even if the good comes slow.

I will withstand all things until the worse of the worse pass me up. know better things has to come.

Day 156

UNDER PLAY for the over play! It was once a police that use to shake everyone down that he came into an encounter with. It was in his mind to take all the contraband from anyone he saw. He was the type of person that was programmed. You can't talk him out of anything. He would lock up his family and friends. When you encounter someone like this you must give them some eye candy for a treat. Leave out something that is little to you or something that you can get back instantly. He would be happy that he found something while he is thinking he hurt you. He didn't know you put the contraband out for him to find so he could feel he did something. All along you had the most valuable things stashed away in safety. Once he found something he'll stop looking for other things.

I will say out a scape goat or a dummy to throw people off from what I truly have or trying to get across.

Day 157

NOTHING LASTS FOREVER! All things will either pass over or pass away one day. Things fade, deteriorate, or get old and wore out. Everything and everybody will come to an end.

Whatever I encounter will be gone one day so I must not get overly caught up in a matter.

Day 158

THERE IS NO big "I" or little "you"! A lot of people consider themselves bigger than the next person. Their conversation is like "I am great but you are small." They tower themselves over everyone else instead of being equal.

I will not see another person as lower than me.

Day 159

LIVE FOR TODAY because tomorrow is not promised! We must make it through the day that we are in before we began focusing on another day. Everything perishes, including life and days. Today is more valuable than another because I know for sure I am alive in it.

I must enjoy my day for it is for that. If I can't have pleasure out of it than I must live accordingly as it is and sea light.

ଓଃଃ୧ଓଃ

Day 160

NEVER GIVE AWAY anything that you cannot stand to lose! It is okay to be free hearted, caring, and to share. But if you can't afford what you are giving out then do not do it.

I will not give away anything that offends me or makes me suffer.

Day 161

WHEN PEOPLE or the things of life resist we must persist! When elements seem as it is pushing or pulling against us. We must stand the challenge and over power it until it gives in. Persistence and consistence run hand and hand. We must not let anything hold us down or hold us back from achieving what we believe in.

I will continue to come back over and over again when there is blockage.

Day 162

MOST OF THE TIME, the people that you bless aren't usually the ones who blesses you back! Our blessings will come from another person that we weren't expecting it from. It's like a substance in a magnetic field that travels invisibly amongst the sect of people with alike endeavors. It may even come in a different way in which we gave out the blessings.

I will not always look for the person whom I blessed to bless me back.

Day 163

MORE LIKE A GHOST! Ghosts are able to slip into places and not be noticed or they can be around people and not be seen. This is an art. People can be in the flesh but overlooked or enter places and be avoided or avoid others.

I don't want to be seen or heard!

Day 164

SIMPLICITY is the essence of complexity! Being simple makes things complicated at times. Some people may be expecting so much more. A lot of people don't understand, simple moods, words or gestures. It irks their nerves.

I must know that being simple is not the remedy at all times.

Day 165

IF YOU WANT CHANGE then you have to change the three most important things: the people around you, the places you go, and the things you do! A lot of people want to change but they don't want to change the people that they hang around. The people that do the things that they want change of will trigger their mind to digress and go in a backwards condition. They will be enticed, peer pressured, and tempted to succumb from evolution.Places draw the same people that will have influences on you. If you want change, then you need a fresh environment, a new look, and new sources. You even feel different when you travel to new places. We have to change the things we do if we want change. The items we have cannot reflect back on what we want to change from. Every object and objective has to transform.

I must change 3 things if I want complete change.

Day 166

I CAN COMPLAIN but I won't because it won't do any good! Complaining is a useless result. Complaining holds you back from doing what you need to do. You waste energy and time complaining when you could have used that energy and time elsewhere. Plus sometimes, complaining only makes things worse.

Instead of complaining, I will utilize my substances more wisely.

Day 167

SOMETIMES, crying means victory and redemption! Crying isn't always the equivalent of pain and suffering. Crying has been said that it cleanses the soul. Crying is also symbolic for tears of joy or overwhelming happiness and break throughs.

I understand that crying is also a good sign.

Day 168

AT TIMES, things happen that only the Lord knows why! When we have no explanation for things that happen in our lives it is not for us to know why. Some knowledge and information is too high for us to understand.

God has reasons for us that I don't know of.

Day 169

SOLITUDE IS NECESSARY for our destiny! All great men have encountered some kind of solitude. Isolation brings you in tune with your complete self. It has you to search and seek for treasures that is deep within your inner being. To be alone is to get to know wonders.

If Dr. Martin Luther King Jr., Malcolm X, Nelson Mandela, Jesus Christ, and Moses the Hebrew went through solitary confinement, then so can I.

Day 170

IF YOU SET an example then others will follow! People imitate without knowing that they are doing it at times. It is like if you sing a catchy song around a person, then minutes later the song will replay in their head, as if it originated from them and before they know it they will be singing the song out loud. When you do certain things people assume that is the way it is supposed to go or either that is the modern day linguistics. People feel that if you could do something then they can also.

Somebody must lead so it might as well be me that set the standards.

Day 171

EVERYTHING that I know was once learned! Ninety percent of all information is knowledge that has been recycled throughout generations. Everything you have thought of has been already thought of by another person. Everything that is said has been already spoken before. Where it be in a different phrase, time frame, or contrast.

To say someone copied, stole a saying, or quote is only my opinion because I don't know who could have said this before me already.

Day 172

THEY SAY THAT MONEY on the wood make the bet look good. But I say any type of gambling is risky. People get hurt all the time because of gambling. When they lose, they are disappointed or may want to cause harm to someone else to get their funds back. Gambling is like a drug that is addiction and destroys families and dreams.

At times, we should take risks to get on top but I must know what I am doing.

Day 173

WHO LEFT YOU to be judge over me? This is the question that you ask hypocrites and self-righteous people. People act like they can form an opinion on another all the time. They criticize or go off of things that is supposedly.

No one that isn't a matter discernment has the right to judge me.

Day 174

RESPECT goes a long way! To get along with others we must respect their differences and similarities of what we harbor. We don't have to be amicable but it is best to respect the space, mind, feelings and actions of others. Respecting people can get you ahead and take you far. You will also find favor.

I don't have to like a person but I still have to respect them.

Day 175

YOU MUST FACE the judgement of your foolishness! When we do simple or foolish things then we must face the consequences of it. We will be handed down discernment for our negligence, goofs, and stupidity.

If I do something foolish than I should not think that I won't pay the price for my foolishness.

Day 176

IT AIN'T NOTHING to it but to do it! Some people act like things are so different or complicated to do. They hesitate and procrastinate instead of just going ahead and doing what needs to be done. People hold themselves back by not doing what needs to be done.

The only thing that is standing in my way is me just doing it.

Day 177

THERE IS STRENGTH in numbers! Have you ever heard the saying that says "together we stand but divided we fall?" that saying is so true. A group of people can do what just one person can't do by their self. Numbers make things happen. When a lot of people get together mountains get moved.

I will unify myself amongst others to get things accomplished.

Day 178

YOU CAN'T BE COOL with everybody! Being friendly with everybody can end up getting you hurt in more ways than one. A lot of people will use you or have other ulterior motives. To be ebullient is for another to misuse or abuse your attributes.

Everybody is not meant to be my friend.

Day 179

ALWAYS KEEP A STASH and a backup plan! There's no telling when a rainy day is going to come your way. No one is exempt from hitting a rough spot in their life. Yet, the ability to bounce back is my planning ahead. You can depend on yourself and have a certain level of comfort by keeping a stash and a backup plan.

I will always keep something put away for hard times.

Day 180

DON'T MISTAKE humbleness for weakness! Some people are humble because of the things that they have been through or because of the things that they don't want to go through. People misconstrue nobleness and modesty as being a person without strength or their own ability to think.

It takes more diligence for me to be humble than raucous.

Day 181

I'D PREFER THE UGLY TRUTH than a pretty lie! People lie a lot of times to make it sound good. Not knowing that even though the truth may hurt it's always the best thing to do. Eventually the truth is going to manifest regardless. When you tell the truth, people can have a chance to decide what they are going to do with the truth. It is not reverent to without information.

I will not leave anyone in the blind.

Day 182

I WOULD IF I COULD but since I can't, then I'm not! People can do only what they are able to do. If it passes their capabilities than that is no way to manage what is proposed. Trying to overdo things will stress you out and leave you with a mission that you can't compete.

I will do all that is in my power to do it but I will not go out of my own way if I believe it is impossible.

Day 183

SOME PEOPLE can't decipher between what's real and it's opposition. So, to say "keep it real" is futile! Most people can't define what's really real. They can state opinions but that doesn't mean it's factual. What's real to another person may not be the meaning of real to you.

To a person that can't distinguish pureness from its difference. I will restrain from entertaining them with a conversation of such.

Day 184

SOME THINGS work themselves out! We worry about our situation that will eventually play out. All we have to do is relax and let things run themselves and take a natural course.

I don't have to always indulge in the affairs of my life. I can just let them flow.

Day 185

SO MANY PEOPLE nowadays are stagnant. Some people don't know being at a standstill or staggering is worse. At least staggering has some type of movement huh? However, my preference is neither. I prefer to continue to elevate. What is going on at the time cannot hold me all the days of my life. It must be some kind of cumulative that comes about.

I must want more than of what is going on right now.

Day 186

DON'T TAKE what everyone says for face value! The word confirmation is a word for a reason. Some people talk out their necks and say what's frivolous. They may also say what they believe is true but it may not be. It is only true in their minds. We have to take it into consideration and do research to find facts. Depending on others words can put you in a terrible spot.

I must find out for myself whether things are accurate or not.

Day 187

THE LONGER YOU WAIT, the farther you will be pushed back! Procrastinating and hesitating will not just have you at a standstill. It will put you behind because while the world is moving forward, it is moving further away from you. So, we shouldn't put ourselves in a situation where we have to rush or end up out of time.

If I don't wait or procrastinate, then I won't have to play catch up.

Day 188

IF SOMETHING is not working out for you then you should improvise! Improvements are always needed where there is lack, kinks, and slacks. Sometimes we must try new ways and new things to make something work out.

I must search and seek for improvement where it's needed.

Day 189

POTENTIAL IS DETERMINED by the assignment that God has given you! Potential is what is in us but hasn't fully manifested as of now. Therefore, our ability and capabilities has been instilled in us since birth. Our potential is great but we must figure out our purpose for living or it will remain latent.

Everyone's assignment for being on earth isn't the same yet I must play my part.

Day 190

JUST BECAUSE something seems right doesn't always mean it is the best choice! What feels right may not be what's right for you. On the other hand, the best decision for you to make may be one that you do not like.

I have to understand that what I may think, feel, or decide may not be what's best for me all the time.

Day 191

IF YOU CAN LOOK UP, you can get up! When the obstacles of life tend to knock you down, if you can muster a victorious thought or see a way out, then there is still hope and salvation for you.

I won't be in despair. I know if there's a will, there's a way.

Day 192

TAKE OFF THE MEAT, then throw away the bones! People give out information, laws, and policies that is not all the way to the max for you. You may agree with ninety percent but disagree with ten percent. Therefore, when you are in organizations, groups, jobs, schools and etc, take out the literature or lesson that is valuable to you than discontinue the rest.

I can take a portion of what I need to use when I need to use it.

Day 193

THE ACRONYM of A.L.I.V.E is Always Live in View of Eternal! To be alive is to live for what's ahead of you. Some people live in the past but that is not good.

I am ALIVE for what's to come.

Day 194

YOU CAN'T UNDO what's been done but you can control what you do from now on! We cannot change something that has already occurred. The best thing to do is learn and improve from what has happened then master what is in front of us.

Once I get light of a matter I know how to deal with it better.

Day 195

DEVELOP STRENGTH from defeat and success from mistakes! When we get beat, we should now know where we need to build up our endurance and abilities. When we make errors, we should know how to correct what was missed.

When I make a mistake, I have to know how to be better in that area. When I lose, I must get better.

Day 196

IT'S NOT ALWAYS about what happened. Most times, it's about what didn't happen! Have you ever had a gut feeling telling you not to do a specific thing or go a special way? When it's over with, you may be stunned because nothing happened. You believed you were headed towards a reward or something. Maybe it was about what didn't happen which brought that feeling about. Perhaps, you would have had a wreck or got into some type of trouble if you didn't obey that perception.

I can't always look for what happens. I must also pay attention to what didn't happen.

Day 197

FAMILY FIRST—family last! Family should be the first people that you break bread with and the last person that you will ever sell out. Everything that you do in between family is to get back to where you began and end. People nowadays treat strangers and friends better than they do their own blood relative. This behavior is not what family should be about.

Everyone has differences so I will set my confusion apart to always be there for my family.

Day 198

BREAK BREAD! There isn't any sense in being stingy. How do you expect to be blessed when you don't share with anybody else? The world is like a magnetic field. What you dish out will be multiplied back to you.

I must be willing to give it when I am able. I will break bread like the disciples did back in Jesus days.

Day 199

EXPECT THE UNEXPECTED! If you are aware of what's not to be perceived then you will never get caught off guard. Miracles and ramifications come when you are not looking for them.

I will always anticipate the maybes of what is and or could not occur.

Day 200

LOVE IS AN ACTION! Love is a form of affection. We don't say it just to say it without any significance. Most people believe love is a noun such as a thing or pronoun, but love is a verb. Love should be showed and not just told.

My love should be expressed as an expression.

Day 201

NEVER go along just to get along! If you don't agree with someone or something then don't make yourself feel bad trying to appease the next person.

I can have disagreement with a person and still get along with them.

Day 202

IT'S OKAY to help people but don't help them to the point where it hurts you! If helping someone by giving them your last piece of bread makes you starve then don't do it.

As long as it does not severely affect me I can help people as long as I like to.

Day 203

YOUR PROSPERITY is directly related to your purpose in life! Wherever your calling is for life, there you will have your gift to bless you all the days of your life. Your financial and mental stimulation is in your reason for living or your repertoire.

I will search to find my talents so I can live extra ordinary.

Day 204

EITHER YOU'RE PART of the problem or part of the solution! There is no in between in solving equations. It's either you do or don't do. Likewise, you don't have a neutral zone for settling disputes. Even if you are quiet and sit through it, you are part of the problem because you didn't help seize it.

I must decide if I should resolve the problem or not.

Day 205

IF YOU WANT things done right, you have to do them yourself! Not many can get things aligned perfectly like you can yourself. You know exactly what you want and how you want it and another person may add their own touch of taste to your flavor.

To avoid arguments and having to have someone do what I want over and over again, I will do it myself.

Day 206

GOOD THINGS come to those who wait! Sometimes, waiting gets you the best of things because the ones that won't wait will run into malfunctions and complications. It's like the saying that says "Patience is a virtue." There is power in waiting until excellence comes your way.

There is nothing wrong with me waiting for something good.

Day 207

IT'S JUST ME being me! You have never walked in my shoes, been where I've been, seen what I've see, or did what I have done. You may not understand things that I say or the things that I do. However, everything that I do and say is out of love. Never have I intentionally meant to be harsh with words or my doings - knowing how strong my words are. The Lord has made me bold for a reason. It's true that I don't know how to deal with sensitive people because I have never been that way. I'm learning and growth is a process and is not at a snap of a finger.

Paul has said he knows how to be weak to the weak and strong to the strong. He knows how to be gentile to the gentiles and a jew to the jews. Unfortunately, I haven't been blessed as of yet to have a chameleon suit, but I do pray for humbleness.

Day 208

BE INTO DEFUSING BOMBS and not setting them off! Anger causes a lot of unnecessary mishaps. When people are like a time bomb, I avoid ticking them off as well as myself. I do what I have to do or say to avoid the conflict.

I'm into settling disputes and not encouraging them.

Day 209

THE EYES are the windows to the soul! People can lie to you with their lips or make you believe their gestures but the eyes tell the truth. If you want to see what's really inside of a person, look into their eyes to search out their most inner and deepest thoughts.

I know that eyes will tell it all.

ଓଃଓଃ

Day 210

A PERSON that will make a fool out of their self just to make you smile is a person that is truly in love with you! People that sacrifice themselves to uplift is an example of a genuine, caring, concerned, and compassionate person. One must pay attention to the affects and signs.

I will never discredit anyone that goes out of the way to put a smile on my face.

Day 211

YOU CAN do all the right things the right way but there is still someone that is going to complain! There is no way that you can please everybody. Somebody is always going to disagree.

I will not let anyone's complaints and grievances affect me.

Day 212

COMMUNICATION IS KEY! Relationships not friendships can last without conversing. Understanding comes by hearing and hearing comes by speaking, communication keeps problems down. What separates humans from animals is our ability to communicate. We must speak to get our point across, function, focus, and learn how to treat each other. Communication is how we learned all we know today, from multiplication and addition, to the mysteries of the world and people within today.

I must utilize my full capacity to communicate.

Day 213

MEMORIES are to be cherished when everything else perishes! People die and material things fade. Events will soon end, places deteriorate, and episodes won't last. The only thing that we can have the longest are the memories of these people, places, or things.

I can recapture whatever I choose to in my memories.

Day 214

WE DON'T have to be on the same page to get along! Everyone isn't always going to have the same opinion as you but that doesn't mean that it has to be conflict in the disagreement.

I can still get along with someone if we don't agree. At least we decided together that we can agree to disagree.

Day 215

GREAT THINGS COME in small packages! We don't have to always look for the biggest prizes or the biggest person. The most extravagant thing you need could be short or small. Just think about what you would want more the box that the jewelry box came in or the box that the ten-karat platinum ring is in? Remember the heart may be more valuable than the leg.

I must see greatness for what it is instead of the size it comes in.

Day 216

THERE ARE PEOPLE who God calls to be planters. God will send them ahead of you to prepare the way for you! If you have a plan but no money, resources, or staff you should proceed with your plan. It could be someone with plenty money waiting on someone to come up with a perfect plan. You should search and seek to find that someone waiting to invest.

Whatever I have to do, I should go ahead and do it. I shouldn't worry about what I lack because what I need is already in front of me and waiting for my arrival.

Day 217

I'D RATHER TRY and fail than never try and never know I could have succeeded! A lot of people don't do things because they believe they can't or because they just don't try for numerous reasons. That is a problem, because if they made an attempt then they could have mastered the task. You defeat yourself when you don't try.

I will make all attempts so I can be sure of the outcome.

Day 218

IT'S ALWAYS a flipside to a token! Nothing is always one-sided. Things may lean more towards one way but it can end with a different story than expected.

I will check to see what's on the other side of the issue.

Day 219

SOME THINGS are not for you to understand! When you understand things you tend to accept them or get curious of what is at hand. A person that wants to understand why a person is a snitch or a homosexual may deal with them in that way they are.

It is food to understand a lot about something it is not just for me to want to know.

Day 220

THINGS MAY GET ROUGH, times may get hard, but you must never give up! No matter what happens or how difficult people or situations are for you, you must never quit or stop doing what is positive. Progression takes time to come. All things are not easy. You must be like the little engine or train that could and say over and over again "I know I Can. I know I can. I know I can."

If I keep going eventually I will succeed.

Day 221

PEOPLE WILL ACT awkward even if you fall! It doesn't matter what position, title, or authority one possesses. You can have all the money and other miscellaneous items that people enjoy. Hating does not come from what you have but who you are. I have seen people with nothing but still get the bad end of the stick.

I must realize that I can be at the top of the world or in a bottomless pit and people will still wrong me.

Day 222

DON'T EXPECT anything for nothing! There are motives behind everyone's intentions. Even if it is an honest act of kindness, people do everything for a reason.

I will look for the matter behind the reception.

Day 223

IT'S NEVER ENOUGH LOVE! You can never love somebody too much. You can change how you treat people to make them better but you can still have your degree of love.

I don't have to take my love away.

Day 224

PATIENCE IS A VIRTUE, but time is an essence! A lot of great things happen within time. Time heals a lot of things and within time stuff is exposed. Time wears the enemy down and help you develop what you need.

I already know that with patience power is created. Time is intrinsic and very valuable to my living conditions, so I must become aware.

Day 225

PRESSURE can do two things: bust pipes or make diamonds! When things have a tight grip on you, it can make you crack like an egg and lose your mind. Pressure can make people do what they wouldn't normally do in their right mind. Sometimes, pressure is that force that will make you learn from the downfalls and become a better successor. It is said that diamonds are found deep inside of the ground. They are covered up with dirt and other debris. Most people wouldn't know if what they found was a diamond because it doesn't look like one until work is done on it. It is a different color and looks like a rock until someone manifests it into what was inside of it.

I must decide if I will let pressure destroy me or make the best out of me.

Day 226

DON'T LET the small objects distract you from the big picture! Some people get disturbed and get their mind off focus. They are blinded by the mediocre things happening in their lives and the things around them that they can't see the major points. Pettiness plays a high quality in this avenue.

I must not get side tracked from greatness or settle for less because I won't ever achieve much if I do.

Day 227

EVERY ACTION causes a reaction! No matter what you do, you will always get a response. Even if no one responded, you still got a response, because your response was no response!

It will always be some kind of conduct, manner, or result in all activities.

Day 228

DON'T DIG A HOLE you can't climb out of! It may take a split second to ignite a flame but forever to put it out. Trouble begins in the blink of an eye but could take years to resolve.

I must avoid trouble at all cost.

Day 229

DON'T MAKE your bed harder than what it already is! Just because you are waist deep in a bad situation doesn't mean that you have to make it worse.

Where there is heat, I will put out the fire and flames.

Day 230

YOU CAN BE either ordinary or extraordinary. It is up to you! Ordinary people are plain and simple, but extraordinary people are unusual, unique, and exceptional. It is up to that specific individual to decide their status.

I must choose whether I want my character open to close.

Day 231

IF IT ISN'T BENEFICIAL, it's artificial! What's not real, appealing, or an addition to what you have going on, it is not meant for you. It will eventually wear you down or break you.

I only need what's natural and genuine.

Day 232

ONE OF THE HARDEST things for people to do is to admit when they are wrong! Rarely do a lot of people accept responsibility for their faults. They will find some way to justify it or avoid it. They don't realize that disclaiming their mishap plays into their integrity.

I will own up to my vices, mistakes, and flaws.

Day 233

JUST BECAUSE something sounds good doesn't mean that it is good! I have seen a lot of food that looks good but doesn't taste good. I have sensed things that smell good but is bad for your health. I have heard people mention things that sound good but the end of it is a road to destruction. Just like good feelings that turned out disastrous. What we call good may not be good at all.

I will not believe people just because they claim something is good. I will have to try it for myself, especially if it sounds too good.

Day 234

UNDER THE BLOOD is a champion, so fight until you feel the joy of victory! Somewhere deep down inside your roots are warriors and soldiers. They were not necessarily on the military battle field, but in the war and struggles of life. You have that line and ability to overcome and conquer your problems, defeat, and mistakes.

I will continue to search down inside me until I find the fight to win.

Day 235

A PERSON that shows that they cannot control their words, shows that they cannot control their self, and therefore are unworthy of respect! Some people don't respect their self so if you show them respect, they will take that as a sign to continue to disrespect you. People that are out of control will end up ruining your mood, character, and day.

I will avoid people that has no self-respect or self-control.

Day 236

YOU WILL NEVER know your true strength until it is tested! We are always talking about what we can't stand and what we can't take. However, we will never know it until we encounter that task. People tend to find out that they are stronger than expected.

Never say what you can't do.

Day 237

JUST BECAUSE we have the same blood does not mean that we are family! Being family comes with morals, ethics, understanding, support, unconditional love, and most of all fellowship. If you don't have any of that then you are just related, but not family.

We may have the same blood pumping through our veins, but if you don't apply the qualities then you are not family.

Day 238

YES AND NO are the two most powerful words you will ever say! You can speak a million words, but yes and no holds the most significance. You can either approve or disapprove the motives in your life. One of these two small words can cause tragic or peace can intervene.

I know that the smallest words have the longest impact.

Day 239

TIMING IS EVERYTHING! The pace that things happen at has a major impact on the results. If you miscalculate something then you may cause havoc to reap upon you.

I must calculate all areas and aspects before I indulge.

Day 240

YOU CAN ONLY be young once but immature forever! It doesn't matter how old you are, you can still act like an adolescent. Your age doesn't determine your maturity. People say they are grown all the time because they pay bills, have children, or out on their own. Yet, your status doesn't make you susceptible.

My actions, personality and thinking skills, dictate my growth and development.

Day 241

YOU DON'T JUST do good things, you do things that are good for your vision! A lot of people do good things that do not have anything to do with their dreams and goals. The energy that they used in other things could have went towards their success. Now don't get me wrong, I am not knocking good deeds because it is always nice be helpful. I am saying that it still could be a good deed if it goes towards your success.

I can still do good things that assist in my achievements at all times.

Day 242

WHEN YOU DISCOVER your dream, you will also discover your ability! We were all born with some kind of talents and skills. It takes a long time for some of us to find them. Most of us never discover them and a few of us locate them immediately. However, when we discover what we were born to do, that ability to master it comes naturally and will most likely provide for us.

I have to search until it takes me to find what I can do at ease.

Day 243

The 3 acronyms of F.E.A.R.

1.) **F**-alse **E**-vidence **A**-ppearing **R**-eal
2.) **F**-orget **E**-verything **A**-nd **R**-un
3.) **F**-ace **E**-verything **A**-nd **R**-ecover

A LOT OF THINGS seem to be tangible or real to us, but it is not actually what it looks like. We tend to get frantic for nothing. Some of us run away from our problems or what we aren't aware of. If we are frightened, we stay away. Even though we may be trembling at the stand up and face it in order recuperate, get back or regain what was lost.

When fear creeps upon me I must be aware of which one out of the 3 of the acronyms the fear is.

Day 244

IF YOU WANT to know where you're supposed to go in life, you have to establish a connection with the person who gave you the assignment! Everyone needs guidance, provision, instructions, and advice. The best way to be pointed towards the right directions is to ask the person that created us and crafted the repertoire that we have.

The molder that molded the mold knows me better than I do.

Day 245

WE MUST KNOW the difference between good and great! There are many that are good at what they do, but only a few are great. For instance, some may argue that Charles Barkley was a good basketball player, but Michael Jordan was great. Drew Brees is a good quarterback, but Tom Brady, Peyton Manning, and Brett Farr are great because they surpass records.

Once I supersede the status of goodness. I travel to twilight zone of greatness.

ଔଔଔ

Day 246

IF YOU'RE ON TIME, you're late! My little sister told me this before and it took me years to catch on to what she actually meant. People we are supposed to be ahead of the games. If we are on time, then we are neck to neck with everyone else. In order to surpass others in life, we have to be like that early bird that got the only worm that was there to get.

In order for me not to be average. I must be in front of everyone else.

Day 247

DON'T TRY to explain and give an answer for everything because you can't explain anything to critics! Have you ever heard the saying that says "Don't cast your pearls to seine because they will trample over it?" A hog wouldn't know how valuable your jewelry is. Likewise, mockers, and thrashers will take you sense for folly.

No matter how wise or important the things are that I have to say, a critic will take it the wrong way. When they are supposed to be optimistic they are pessimistic.

Day 248

BEWARE OF DREAM SELLERS! I know a guy that will promise people something one week but they will never get what he promised. Then the next week he will promise another person to do a good deed. Likewise, the second person never received what was promise. Do you think by his reputation that he will ever come through with his promises?

I must know that people that sell dreams are like having false hope.

Day 249

IF YOU LIKE IT, I love it! Sometimes, people can fall in love with things and other people for the simple fact that someone they know likes it or them. It may not have been specifically your style at first, but you will try it for the likes of someone close you to.

Just because I didn't initiatively like something does not mean I can't grow to love it, because someone that I like, likes it.

Day 250

NEVER SPIT where you lay your head! Some people always cause problems where they stay which is why they are never calm and modest. One must keep foolishness and turmoil away from their living quarters.

I will never bring trouble to where I live.

Day 251

STAY IN YOUR LANE! Don't get off track with anybody or allow them to misuse or abuse you. When individuals stay in line then everything will run smoothly.

I will not engage in any foul play.

Day 252

A LOT OF THINGS are simple, but we complicate them! Some people will take simple things as a one plus one addition problem and turn it into an algebra equation.

I will not add nor take away any necessities to anything.

Day 253

THERE IS NO PROGRESS without struggle! Everybody in some form or shape must put forth some kind of effort, strength, or muscle if they want to see flourishing results. No matter how hard the push or pull, one must continue to thrive. If you ever heard of "no pain, no gain," then you know exactly what I mean.

Every day, I will move towards the mark to reach my dreams, goals, or vision. I understand that hardship will come. However, I must endure through it all.

Day 254

ONLY GOD can make a way out of no way! We have all gotten to that point where we feel there is or was no way out of situation we are in our life. When things seem impossible then we must turn it over to a higher power.

Where there is no road, avenue, or channel to escape, then I must give it to the Most High.

Day 255

TAKE NOTHING FOR GRANTED! A lot of people think that others owe them or they are entitled to this or that. So, they brush off others actions or show little to no concern. They think what is already there will be there for as long as they like. They are unaware that items, as well as love, fades away. People will not always treat you the same. Views and thoughts change when we don't acknowledge them.

I must be thankful and grateful of every small and big thing in my life as well as the people surrounding me.

Day 256

EVERYTHING THAT GLITTERS isn't gold! Some people and things appear what they are not. They have a certain element or characteristic that they throw out there to convince, manipulate, or persuade others. I call them imposters, charlatans, and fakes.

If someone or something looks a certain way, I must consider that it may not be the way it looks.

Day 257

THE GRASS isn't always greener on the other side! We as humans believe that life would be better or different if we were with another person or living another person's life. That person we want may be as miserable or more worse off than the one that we are already with. Perhaps, the life that we want to live may drive us crazy or just not be for us. Instead of jumping shifts, we have to make the best out of what we have. We don't need someone else's green gas. All we have to do is make our grass greener than what it already is.

I can brighten up my situation, lifestyle, or relationship near to perfection.

Day 258

GET WHAT YOU CAN while you can for as long as you can! Some people tend to get something and expect for what they have to always be there. Unfortunately, things run out. Things fade and people change. Not only does their mind change, but also how they do things. This is why we must get what's necessary in abundance.

I will drink from the well until it run dry.

Day 259

ALWAYS REMAIN open minded to necessities because being closed minded will have you optionless! We tend to rule out people and events before it happens. Too many times we have lost out like this. We need to start leaving reason and understanding open as oppose to neglecting and ostracizing them.

Sometimes I need a new look on things instead of what's on my mind.

Day 260

NOTHING is without meaning! Everything people do, say, or sign has some type of significance to it. Even when people don't do a thing or don't say anything has a substance to it. Everything that is made signifies something. Every item, element, or formation has sense to someone.

I must find the quality in everything.

Day 261

WE ALREADY KNOW that closed mouths don't get fed but sometimes open mouths don't either. Just because we ask for something doesn't mean we will get a favor in return.

I shouldn't always expect what I ask for. True enough, I may get it most of the times, but not all the time.

Day 262

THE BIRTH of a miracle is surrounded by great obstacles! Don't think it's all bad because of the heartache and pain that you are going through. Know that one must endure the hardship of a battle in order to win, conquer, and overcome.

I know in the misdt of all my problems, that if I watch, endure, and be patient, that supernatural blessing will occur.

ଓଃଌଌଓ

Day 263

IT'S HARD BUT IT'S FAIR! This is the saying that you quote when hardship occurs but you know that you are the reason for the hardship. This is what you declare when the hardship is necessary to achieve a greater good, like building a house or exercising.

It is true that with no pain there will be no gain.

Day 264

IT'S SAD, but it's true! It saddens us a lot to deal with what is true. For example, like a death in the family, the bogus actions of individuals, and the crime rates and sickness.

No matter how sad it is, whatever I have going on, I must realize that it is true.

Day 265

I HEAR a lot of women talking about they are a bad chick this and dad chick that but karma the baddest female I know! Karma is like boomerang. Whatever you dish out will eventually come back to you. The only difference is that karma catches you off guard when you least expect it. So be careful of the wrong that you do because karma is a hunter that seeks revenge.

It is true that what comes around goes around.

Day 266

ONE MUST KNOW the difference between wisdom and knowledge! A lot of people truly believe that wisdom and knowledge is the same thing but it's not, even though both are perspicaciously on intelligence levels. Knowledge is literally information or literature, but wisdom is to handle awareness wisely. A book has information but that doesn't mean the book is wise. A camera and tape recorder has knowledge on it but that does not mean that cameras and tape recorders understand the knowledge on it. This is why smart people do foolish things. The smart person has knowledge but they don't know how to utilize the knowledge. A person can have the knowledge of how to build a microwave, but if they don't know how to use the microwave then they are not wise. They only have the knowledge, but not the wisdom of the appliance. I can give you a blueprint of the circuits to build a cellular phone. The blue print only gives you the knowledge but if you never use a cellular phone then you're ignorant to the usage.

Wisdom is simply knowing what to do with the knowledge that I have attained. I can read several books with knowledge in it, but if I don't apply the knowledge then I am not wise.

Day 267

DON'T GET INVOLVED with every invitation! We shouldn't always be willing to get in another person's affairs. Their business is their business and our business is our business. Most of all, you don't always know who's involved and their state of mind may be detrimental. When we get in other's affair we invite them to ours. We shouldn't accept the offer of going places with different people. It could put us in danger or destroy our image.

I will carefully choose the invitation that I'm offered.

Day 268

CARRY YOURSELVES like gentlemen and scholars! The true definition of men is being tainted by the mass majority image. We no longer open doors for women. We do not use humbleness or politeness. Our intelligence has been replaced by ignorance, greed, selfishness, and deceit. We now have to change our role back to rulers, leaders, and men of our world. Most of all, we must make wise decisions.

I must always present myself with integrity and dignity.

Day 269

LIVE THE REST of your life with no regrets! If I'm ashamed of something, then I shouldn't do it. Nor am I'm going to deny a fact. Resent from your actions. If you are to do it then do it, but if you are not to do or say a thing, then don't.

I can't live my life saying what I could have, would have, or should have done.

Day 270

ALL THOUGHTS have a tendency to clothe itself in its physical equivalent! Your hidden thoughts and secrets of your heart will eventually manifest. Sometimes it comes out accidentally, like during an outburst. Other times, it seeps its way to the surface but all thoughts will come to the light.

It's true that "As a man thinketh so is he."

Day 271

THE LONGEST JOURNEY begins with a single step! No matter how far you have to go in life to achieve your accomplishments. You have to initiate the first step. The more steps you take then the closer you will reach you mark.

I must start all processes out the beginning.

Day 272

GOD HAS PUT SO MUCH in you that if you are willing to capture it, nothing can stop you! We have unknown power that is waiting to be revealed to us. This is what normally happens when we master a task or do a specific thing that we didn't know.

If I am willing to tap into this virtue that the Most High stored into me then I will be invincible.

Day 273

IF YOU PUSH A MULE, nine times out of ten you may get kicked in the grill! A mule is a stubborn, hard headed, or adamant person. The more you attempt to push them into progression, the more you end up getting frustrated or attacked by them. A mule of a person doesn't want to learn and have zero understanding. Most times you will be just wasting time by dealing with them.

I refuse to push a mule.

Day 274

EVEN THOUGH you can do anything in life, the only things that you should master are the things that will take you to your goal! Now I'm not saying don't do mediocre things. Anything that may have the slightest significance is relevant to you. I am merely saying that majority of our time should be devoted to what we want to accomplish.

I must spend my time becoming excellent at what involves my goals.

Day 275

SILENCE speaks volumes! At times, being quiet is more powerful than words. Holding your tongue and peace has more of an impact than a thousand sentences.

I must know when to keep quiet.

Day 276

MOST OF US know the difference between right and wrong. Therefore, your greatest challenge is not in choosing between good or bad between good and best! To do good is one thing but to do your best is another. We must strive for excellence.

I will do better than good. I will always do my best.

Day 277

SUCCESS is largely a matter of adjusting one's self to the ever-varying and changing environments of life, in a spirit of harmony and poise! To things and age changes we must adapt calmly and not panic. Every day new trends and eras come so we must face them head on.

To be a successor I must cope and evolve.

Day 278

A REAL FIGHTER doesn't wear his medals on his chest, he wears them on his back. Only a few people will know what it took for you to achieve your vision. You must be willing to take the scars if you want to wear the crown! It is okay to receive people hearts in a physical combat. The most difficult battles are the ones that you fight with yourself and the war of good versus evil. The scars that we wear on our minds, souls, spirits, gadgets, and backs will be known by not very many. Once we overcome and endure while still going through the most precious crown that we wear is invisible to must but god and our close ones see it.

Everybody doesn't have to know what all I have been through as long as my love ones and I know.

Day 279

OUR HABITS RULE US! Most people cannot contain their habits. The habit or habits dictate what we do, what we think, and how we feel.

I must regain control of my habits.

Day 280

YOU WEREN'T DESIGNED to have too much or too little but you were designed for God's purpose! Today, people are too caught up in what they have or what they do not have. Our worth has been dictated by the merchandise, money, or spouses in our lives. However, this is not what life is all about. We are here on earth to find one reason for living and complete our mission.

I will locate my destiny and fulfill exactly that.

Day 281

IT'S GOOD to be outspoken but somethings should kept to yourself! Negative thoughts and things that will hurt others or affect you in the long run should not be heard.

I must know when to keep my mouth close.

Day 282

WE MUST BE CAREFUL of the company we keep around because we can end up being guilty by association! You may not understand why someone may not like you or mistreat you for some unknown reason. People tend to judge us and view us as the people we hang around. When a person views us as the people we hang around, if we are around a known thief then others will have a close look out on us when we come around their merchandise.

I reflect my association as well as they reflect me.

Day 283

CORRECT ME if I'm wrong! A lot of people don't like to be corrected so they feel intimidated, insulted, or get mad when one modifies them.The thing about corrections is that you will rather be right than wrong even if it is getting learned at your expense. I would not want to go through life thinking things is right when they are not.

I do not want to be ignorant of a thing, so correction is necessary.

Day 284

IF SOMETHING has been working out for you then keep doing it don't change up! Too many times have I seen people change what has been benefiting for them. Then when they change for the normal course they wonder why they are failing. For instance: I have seen people run plays in sports that gets them ahead than all of a sudden. The coach changes the plays or takes the people out the game that was winning for them. Then this is when they begin losing.

I must keep everything the same when it is working out for me.

Day 285

WHATEVER YOU DO or whatever happens just do no panic! I have had several car wrecks but still manage to control the motion of the car. Even if I'm approaching a potential wreck, I avoid it calmly. My mom asks me how do I do these things because she would be frightened. I always say if something is going to happen then it is going to happen any way so the best way to handle it is to not panic during the transaction. If someone is a server in a restaurant and orders happen to get backed up, the average person will tend to begin dropping things because they are in a rush. A cook may even burn the food up because their mind is going bizarre. You should never panic. Just be calm and everything will slowly but surely progress.

To avoid the inevitable, I must eliminate fear.

Day 286

IF YOU DO SOMETHING consciously ninety-nine times, on the one hundredth attempt, you wouldn't have to force yourself or try because it would have become a habit by then! My mother, Mary taught me the above quote a long time ago. For example, if you had to think about exercising every day for ninety-nine days straight, when you wake up on the one hundredth day, you wouldn't even have to think about exercising. You will automatically wake up and do it.

I must program my body and mind to get use to what I want it to.

Day 287

DON'T GET CAUGHT UP! We must not get caught up in schemes, bad affairs, nor mischief. We must avoid such heinous obstacles by all cost.

It's true that I can occasionally do what I choose to do but in all my doing I must not get caught.

Day 288

THROW IT IN THE GUTTER and get another! We must not hesitate to throw away what distracts us or keep us from our goals. We should regard what is old and useless as trash.

Eventually I will get something or someone that is new and better.

Day 289

PEOPLE WILL throw you under the bus to save their life! What I mean by saving their life is their image, expectations, and dignity. I have seen people use other people names to clear their own up or use somebody else as a cover up.

I refuse to give anyone the leverage to throw me out there.

Day 290

YOU DON'T HAVE TO understand what's understood! If you already know something then you shouldn't have to go back and forth with it. Once an understanding is met there is no need to reiterate the facts.

What I already understand doesn't have to be refined.

Day 291

BY ANY MEANS necessary! What we have to get accomplished must be done by all cost if the risk doesn't cause a transgression.

Whatever it is for me to do must be handled with no exceptions.

Day 292

WE WILL GO THROUGH ups and downs like a roller coaster but we must manage through it all! Times can be tough or easy depending on the situation. No matter what occurs we should cope with it. Changes will happen so stand firm and hold on.

I must survive through the ins and outs.

Day 293

SOME PEOPLE can't do wrong in my eyesight! Have you ever heard the saying "Even if they are wrong they are right?" This is the case with loved ones such as my mother. No matter what she does, she is accurate and adequate in my eyesight.

To my love ones that are superior, I must read just my thoughts and actions to see things their way.

Day 294

YOU CAN NEVER get too comfortable! When people get overly comfortable they tend to slip and slack up. Being too comfortable makes you cause mistakes and get lazy or be unprepared.

I must be on point at all time.

Day 295

YOUR FAITH will be tested by your fate! The way that you react to tests, temptation, and trials in your life determines the outcome of you the way you live.

My fortune and future events is dictated by whether I stand firm or not.

Day 296

DON'T LET anybody take you fast! People try to coerce or persuade a person by doing things or asking them something before they are able to think. Therefore, later when you reflect, you figure out that what occurred shouldn't have. People will volunteer you.

Always take the time to think before acting towards someone else.

Day 297

IGNORANCE is bliss! People have the wrong definition of the word ignorance. They think ignorance means you are stupid or not as smart. The word ignorance actually means you don't know something. It's not a bad word like people make it sound. If you weren't a politician, you would be ignorant of politics or if you weren't the lawyer or doctor, you would be ignorant of law and medical terms. At times , it's good to not know something.

It is all right for me not to know something because I am better off not knowing certain stuff.

Day 298

KNOW WHEN to be aggressive! Occasionally, we have to put our foot down. Rarely do people hear the kindness of a heart.

The only way to get my point across at times is to be tough.

Day 299

DOWN BY LAW! When I say someone is down by law, it means that particular person is with you against all odds. It is in their nature to be by your side.

I need people that will be riders regardless of what's going on and I will be equivalent to them.

Day 300

THE ONLY THING worse than not thinking at all is thinking too much! When you over think a situation you begin to see and assume things that are not there. Hallucinations and delusions come with thinking too much and your mind becomes exhausted.

I know that I must think pass average but when I go overboard than I am out of line.

Day 301

SOMETIMES, no news is good news! It is a good thing not to hear from people at times. I have seen events where the only information was heard came from a bearer of bad news. Even if you are waiting on a job or an answer pertaining to business it is good for the time being because you didn't yet deny so patient.

When I don't hear from anyone. I can at least say I haven't heard bad news.

Day 302

KNOW WHEN to turn a death ear! Everything is not meant for you to hear. We have to tune things out at times. We can avoid getting hurt and hurting others by ignoring statements.

I can pick certain things out that I want to hear.

Day 303

DON'T LET anybody but you in the trick bag! I have seen people offer others gifts and bribes then turn around and black mail them for their position for accepting the contraband. A lot of bogus people will set you up and frame you.

Just because someone seems like there is no ulterior motive behind their gestures don't always believe them.

Day 304

CONFIRMATION is a wonderful essence! It's tough to believe what only one person says but when two or three agree with the one then it is confirmed and may be reliable.

Don't go ahead with the process of a thing until it has been confirmed.

Day 305

NEVER go against the grain! Going against the grain is like getting a bad haircut or drinking ice cold coffee. If a thing is not meant to go that way, then be accurate and adequate.

Whatever I do I must do it properly.

Day 306

PLAY FOR KEEPS! If you play a game, gamble, or bet always be in the mind that whatever you end up with at the end must be worth your while. Even when people are not serious you can joke and play but not be careful of the outcome.

Even when I play I must play to capture.

Day 307

THERE'S no love lost! Just because you have an altercation with someone and you get in your feelings that does not mean you should lose love for that person. You can get mad at someone but not hate them.

My love will remain no matter what happens.

Day 308

PRESENTATION and delivery of a message is everything! It doesn't matter who you are or what you are saying at times. If you do not present the delivery of your message properly then the person won't get it.

What I am saying can mean a lot but have no value if I can't get someone interested in what I'm saying.

Day 309

DO what's best for you! You can't always attempt to please everyone else. You have to satiate and find time for yourself.

When it comes down to deciding between individuals or a group, I have to do what's best for me.

Day 310

RARELY go backwards! When you go backwards, it's normally because you left something behind. When we backtrack, our forward progress stops. It is good to look towards the future instead of living in the past. We can still have love for people; but still, we must move on.

I will not back track unless it's absolutely necessary.

Day 311

MIND your own business! The time and effort that is spent dabbing our nose in other's business can be spent on expanding and advancing on our own. We drain energy minding other folk's business. A lot of problems can be avoided by minding your own business as well.

I know that the world can be a happier place if everyone minds their own business.

Day 312

TRUTH is the safest ground to stand on! We have less to worry about when we speak truth. We have to cover up lies with other lies when we lie. To avoid problems, focus on what's factual.

The reverse is that I will lie to only save my life and my love ones.

Day 313

IT IS NOT UNTIL the heat is turned up and the burner is on that our true character will reveal itself! Some people don't know what's instilled in them until they are put in an awkward situation. Then they do and say things that they have never done or said before.

My true identity will eventually come out.

Day 314

PRIDE will cause harm to yourself and others! Arrogance and cockiness will have you missing out on good chances with exhilarating people. Pride will cause you to turn down what you desperately need. Your pride will also make others want to do something bad to you.

I must relinquish my pride.

Day 315

THERE IS NO USE in crying over spilled milk! As the old saying goes. What has already happened is over with. It is not good to bring up what is finished.

I will not fuss over what has been ruined, broken, or dismantled.

Day 316

IF YOU'RE NOT with me, then you are against me! Have you ever heard this saying? People that are not on my team are the opposition. There is no in-between. Either you are on my side or you're not.

I must recognize the people that are with me.

Day 317

ALWAYS work on yourself! You can't possibly be anything to anyone else if you can't be the best you can be for yourself first. Never stop improving.

I must get myself together before I can help anyone else.

Day 318

IF YOU PLAY with a child of god, then God is going to play with you! A lot of people mistreat God's children, then they wonder why bad things happen to them. We must watch how we treat God's people because God will return that anguish back upon you ten times worse.

My God will take care of the ones who misuse me.

Day 319

STOP adding fuel to the fire! When people are already frustrated from words, their best way to avoid combustion is to not say anything that will send them over the edge. When people are already under pressure, don't apply any more. That is like jumping out of a frying pan into a skillet.

I know when enough is enough.

Day 320

IT POURS when it rains! One moment, everything can be going good, then the next minute, life can go all the way sour. Attacks after attacks may happen to us. Things can go from sugar to dirt within minutes.

I must be aware that problems will build up on me.

Day 321

ALL THINGS come to an end! No matter how hard things seem right now, we must know eventually that it will pass by. Even the good times will one day cease. All material things, objects, elements, substances, relationships, and friendships will end.

I know that nothing lasts forever.

Day 322

RUMORS are only to be taken into consideration...If even that at all! Rumors can end up being either true or false. Many rumors aren't to be taken for face value until it has been confirmed repeatedly, even then, it may still whine up being not true at all.

I know rumors get started for many reasons, so I will not be quickly enthused by them.

Day 323

A LOT OF THE TIME, it's not about what you have or what has happened to you. It's about what you didn't get or what didn't happen to you! A lot of us look for good things to happen to us and for us. But we fail to realize that even if something bad didn't happen to us, then that is still a good thing.

I should be thankful that nothing bad happened.

Day 324

SOMETIMES, we have to think for others! We can't get mad at every little thing people do. Sometimes they are dormant so we have to step in and give them guidance. When they are not acting, or talking appropriate, then we must take control and lead them. It's like when we are on the road and driving a car. We must drive for ourselves and others that are also on the road. We may have to step on brakes when someone else runs a light.

I have to obtain charisma to think for the others.

Day 325

AIN'T NO half-stepping! When you step to someone, it is best to come correct. Don't stop at mid-range doing anything. Either go all the way or none at all.

Whatever I do, I must fully exhaust my remedies.

Day 326

IT'LL DAWN on you! Whatever you don't know will eventually come to the light. You may be unaware of many things, but one day the switch to the light bulb will come on.

People that are incognizant are to be told it'll dawn on you.

Day 327

IT IS EASIER to get into trouble than is to get out of trouble! It takes only a few seconds to get into major trouble, but years to resolve. Mistakes, mishaps, and mischief are easily entertained in a blink of an eye, but people may never get out of it.

I must avoid trouble by all cost.

Day 328

WHAT GOD HAS for me is for me! The things you go through were not designed for anybody else. They were specifically tailor-made to fit your life. God knows us better than we know ourselves so what he creates for us is to make us learn, identify and make us better, stronger, and wiser.

I must not look at other folk's lives and wonder what is happening to me isn't happening to them.

Day 329

TRUE PROSPERITY means to be free of worry and fear! To be prosperous reflects on a state of contentment and knowing that everything necessary is being taken care of.

I must know prosperity is an inner security instead of outer.

Day 330

THE ONLY THING that has power over you is the thing that you allow to have power over you! Nothing has complete virtue unless you submit. Acceptance plays a major part in power.

If I don't want something to have power over me, then I must refuse.

Day 331

DON'T BE ENTERTAINED when people throw our camera shots! People say camera shots because they don't have the heart to say what they want to say directly to you. A camera shot is when people sing a song or rap that is really being directed towards you or they say something out of a movie or quote a quote instead of being up front. They may even speak in third person or act like they are talking to themselves but they are actually relating to you.

I don't pay attention to camera shots because that is cowardly.

Day 332

WE JUST DON'T receive medals from God, we earn them! I know it feels good to gain free things but it feels even better to earn them. God put us through tests to receive our rewards. When we earn things, we become worthy.

It is okay to earn medals instead of just getting them freely from God.

Day 333

IF YOU CHANGE the way you think then your behavior will change. Once your behavior changes then your actions will change then your lifestyle will change by you leading an example with your own lifestyle then the people that are around your lifestyle will change. If you want others to change then you must have to be a better influence. By starting with the way you actually think will create a great evolution with another person as well as yourself.

If I want a better life than I have to change my actions, behavior, and thinking ability.

Day 334

RESPECT goes a long way! Certain people die or even kill because of disrespect. Disrespect causes bad attitudes and harsh words. On the other hand, respectful people can be invited anywhere and have a nice time. Respect makes you get along with anyone. Nobody really wants to be around a disrespectful person but respect earns your promotions and rewards.

I will succeed in life more by being respectful with manners than being disrespectful.

Day 335

ALWAYS remain well rested! You cannot really focus properly if you are tired, exhausted, and worn out. You will be dysfunctional if you don't get the required rest that your body and mind needs.

No matter what happens in my life, I must make sure that I rest so that my body or mind won't shut down. I have to be able to have a clear mind to deal with the problems of this crooked world.

Day 336

EVERYBODY has a pattern! Everyone has a specific way of doing things whether they realize it or not. If you figure this pattern out you will know what to expect and how to deal with them. You will also know how to defend yourself and counter attack.

I know that everyone is made up with a pattern in how they do things. Even if they change up the current pattern, their next pattern can be figured out.

Day 337

GIVE IT to them in the raw! Most people don't take heed to vague instructions and advice. Beating around the bush don't get to them as laying things straight across the wood. Also simplicity can be undermined or misunderstood, we have to be direct and upfront.

Uncut should be more knowledge, pure, and easier to construct to me.

Day 338

SHOOT your jumper! We have to make an attempt on whatever we want accomplished. If we want to be with someone then we must make an approach. If we want a job than we must fill out an application and do follow up calls. Whatever we aim for should be challenged whether we fail or miss the opportunity. Just like in basketball when you shoot the ball you miss or you might hit. You will never know until you take the chance. This is the same in life, circumstances, and situations.

I have to put my bid in.

Day 339

YOU CAN'T BE FRIENDLY with everyone! Some people will take your kindness for weakness. Being friendly with everyone can get you hurt or leave you in a bad situation.

I have to put my guards up at times.

Day 340

AGREE TO DISAGREE! It is not arguing nor feuding when you are not on the same page. It is simply disagreeing yet actually in reality your kind of disagreeing in a peculiar way because you agreed to have your differences between each other.

I can politely agree to disagree with someone.

Day 341

AVOID FIGHTS! Only animals are unable to communicate properly to the point that they can't work their problems out. Humans have the highest level of intelligence and communication, so when we fight amongst each other it's like looking at two rams banging their heads against each other in combat.

I look less than a human when I stoop so low as to fight stupidity.

Day 342

ALL FIGHTS result down to only 3 things: sexual Competition, religion, and economics! People fight for many reasons but the root of the problem comes for only 3 main things. For instance: If you argue with someone because they bumped into you or said something out of the way,you only indulge in the combat because of your belief, money problems, or what the opposite sex will think of you. Countries are fighting today in war because of different religions. The world goes to battle for oil, diamonds, and gold which is economics. Others fight to impress the opposite sex or they will go off because they are sexually frustrated.

No matter what is covering up the root of the problem, I must discover one of the three reasons behind it and not only see the cover up.

Day 343

NO CROSS. No crown! If you don't go through what is required to gain honor then you will never receive the crown. We must endure cross outs, cover ups, and the penalty of being nailed to a cross like Jesus Christ to manifest our glory.

I know that in order to wear the crown I must endure the cross

Day 344

NEVER dwell on negativity! When we let negativity take us over than we suffer from pain, anxiety, stress and depression. Negative things and thoughts will also make us hallucinate. Therefore, I must avoid negativity by all cost if I want to live a peaceful, calm, and glorious life.

I must turn a negative into a positive.

Day 345

REMAIN SUCKER FREE in order to be drama free! Don't let nobody sike you up because you can end up being set up for failure like that. To be a sucker is to be left with a dumb founded look on your face. A sucker always gets the bad end of the stick. People will misuse and abuse a sucker. Being around a sucker is just as bad. They will rub unintentional drama off on you.

I will stay away from suckers as well as not be one.

Day 346

CRUEL and unusual punishment shouldn't be wished on our worse enemy! I was listening to a radio station once and the host was asking people was the nutri-loft cruel and unusual to give to inmates in prison. Now nutri-lost is called gruel. It is all kind of food stuck together than turned into a brick like tasteless substance.However, shockingly 70% of the people said they didn't have any love for inmates. What's amazing to me is that they don't even know the inmates. The inmates could have been innocent and falsely accused. They could have changed their lives into being righteous or they could have another side to the story that differ from yours. The thing is that if you wish cruelty to someone else then you are just as bad as them. You are no better than the next person. At the end of the day, wrong is wrong without a scale.

No matter what has happened I will not wish nor repay evil for evil.

CSEDSOCR

Day 347

DON'T CATCH stage fright when the stage becomes too big for you! I see ball players get all the way to finals and freeze up and do poorly because it's their first time being there. I have seen orators become nervous and fidget because they are put in front of a larger audience that they have never been placed in before. I have seen people act goofy, clumsy, forget words, or break things in the eye sight of another person that they secretly admire.

I will not get bubble guts when I experience something uncomfortable or unknown.

Day 348

DON'T BE MISLED or deceive yourself because everybody needs somebody! I hear a lot of individuals saying they don't need anyone and how much they are okay with their self. Now it is cool to be independent and confident in yourself. Yet, at times people are here to assist us and console us at times of need. We can't get everything accomplish by ourselves.

I know fellowship is required.

Day 349

A PERSON that brings a bone will carry a bone! People that bring you conversation about a particular person will take what you say and carry it to another person. In many cases this is called two-faced. However, when they carry the message it will have more dirt added on the bone than from when it started.

I can't trust a gossiper.

Day 350

DON'T ALLOW anyone to force you out of your character! We jump out of our element so quickly before we notice it. We end up cussing when we normally don't, fight when we are a natural lover, or do and say something that we totally regret.

I must keep my cool at all times.

Day 351

A MAN IS ONLY as strong as his woman! A man is naturally masculine but his woman pushes him further. Your soulmate is your inspiration and aspiration. She gives you that drive and extra force that you need to excel and succeed abundantly. If your woman has no charisma, ideas, true love, and influence then she may bring you down lower from the point where you are.

I must choose my significant other wisely.

Day 352

TREAT YOURSELF. Don't beat yourself! I have seen a lot of people sell themselves short. They don't believe they deserve more than what they already have. They think negative and beat themselves down. We have to enjoy our life while we can. We must take care of ourselves and show love and support to our self. There is nothing wrong with being certain with yourself.

Know your worth!

Day 353

LOOK ALIVE! I see people looking down and depressed like they don't have any life in them. The glow has been taken out of their eyes. It's is not good to look dead. You feel better when you're jolly and more people will be drawn to you that way.

I vow to be lively.

Day 354

IF YOU'VE NEVER been where you've been, then you will never get to where you're going! We all have a destiny as well as destination. However, the places and circumstances we have already traveled gave us the drive to get elsewhere.

I must keep going until I get to where I need to be.

Day 355

IF YOU ARE ASHAMED of something then don't do it! I have seen a lot of people doing things that embarrasses them and they later regret it. If they could have avoided the incident or accident then they would be better off. Yet, pride and unawareness usually have us go ahead and do shameful things.

I will not do anything that will later make me ashamed.

Day 356

REPETITION may be annoying but in certain situations it is necessary! Repeating things have the tendency to lock it into your brain. Reiteration is a great way to memorize things. When You constantly do something over and over it becomes a habit.

Drilling things like a drill sergeant isn't always bad.

Day 357

IT'S NOT what you do it's how you do it! You can do a million things but if you do it at ease then people will respect you and honor you more than making it seem complicated. The way you do things is always being watched more than what you are actually doing.

I must plan and execute carefully how I do things.

Day 358

WHEN YOU CAN'T deal with it then bounce like a bad check! We don't have to put up with people nor situations that we don't want to deal with. When it comes to this then we can leave the scene or compel them to leave.

I can ignore what I don't won't to deal with or delete it.

Day 359

DON'T LET ANYBODY pick you like a combination to a lock! People are always fishing for information. They will throw out keywords or statements so that you will latch on to it like a fish on a hook. We must not go for such picking. They may be trying to pick us for money, food, clothing, and etc. These people are con-artists and manipulators.

I refuse to be picked.

Day 360

BY CHOICE or force! People must get in compliance by either force or choice. Either they choose to do something on their own free will or they a forced, persuaded, or peer pressured.

It can either be by force or choice, but I know people will fall in suit.

Day 361

IN ORDER TO LEAD you must first follow! No one comes out of their mother's womb and instantly know how to lead. A leader must be molded, shaped and developed. It takes time, experience, and interest and wisdom to become a shepherd.

It is impossible knowing something without learning, seeing, or hearing it first.

Day 362

IF YOU WANT THINGS done right, then it is best to do it yourself! Nobody can have that exact touch like you. Not too many people know how you like things done so do it yourself to show them first and then they will learn. By doing things yourself it keeps problems down.

I can count on myself to get it done right.

Day 363

I'M TOO FAST for a slow conversation! A lot of people talk and think they are actually talking over your head but they are not. Then, some people talk beneath you so your attention span is low. Whatever the case may be let them know you are too fast for a slow conversation.

On the other hand, some people are too slow for a fast conversation, so I must tone it down for them.

Day 364

THANKS but no thanks! You can be grateful for someone's offer, but you don't have to accept it. Someone once wanted to assist me in legal issues but I didn't want the help for personal reasons because their help may have turned bad or into an ultimatum.

I don't always have to accept the aid of someone but I can be glad they offered it.

Day 365

I GAVE YOU too much credit! You can expect too much out of people and end up getting let down. You can assume someone's ability and capabilities but your assumption does not hold up. You can depend on someone and wind up empty and void.

I must give credit only when credit is due.

A Letter to My Readers

Dear Readers,

I am an innocent man who has been wrongly convicted of a murder that occurred on Halloween night in 2007 on Stanton Road in Little Rock, AR. If you can assist in any way with the help of my appeals or if you have any information regarding the incident or the actual perpetrators involved, please contact me via the information provided below.

Anything will be helpful and will remain confidential at your request. My family has prepared a REWARD for those who come forth with helpful information.

With sincerest gratitude,
Rahsaan Taylor

Justice for Rahsaan
c/o Rahsaan Taylor
P.O. Box 193302
Little Rock AR, 72219
alphaomegamk2@gmail.com
(501) 541-9279

For more information, visit:
Facebook.com/JusticeforRahsaan

Contact the Author

Send all fan mail, pictures, and ideas,
or comments to:

Rahsaan Taylor ADC# 147955
P.O. Box 500
Grady, AR 71644

I would love to hear from you! Your decisions, thoughts, and comments are very valuable to me.

Maybe we can get together and write a book or maybe your recommendations can inspire me to write another book of any kind.

-Rahsaan

J. KENKADE
PUBLISHING

www.ingramcontent.com/pod-product-compliance
Lightning Source LLC
LaVergne TN
LVHW011154080426
835508LV00007B/406

* 9 7 8 1 9 4 4 4 8 6 6 0 0 *